Through
ENGLISH

By
Ajay Kumar Bhalla

GOODWILL PUBLISHING HOUSE®
B-3 RATTAN JYOTI, 18 RAJENDRA PLACE
NEW DELHI - 110008 (INDIA)

Published by
GOODWILL PUBLISHING HOUSE®
B-3 Rattan Jyoti, 18 Rajendra Place
New Delhi-110008 (INDIA)
Tel. : 25750801, 25820556
Fax : 91-11-25764396
E-mail : goodwillpub@vsnl.net
website : www.goodwillpublishinghouse.com

Printed at :-
Mehra Offset Press, Delhi.

INDEX
(विषय सूची)

AT A GLANCE

INDEX
(विषय सूची)

AT A GLANCE

INDEX
(विषय सूची)

AT A GLANCE

INDEX
(विषय सूची)

AT A GLANCE

INDEX
(विषय सूची)

AT A GLANCE

INDEX
(विषय सूची)

AT A GLANCE

INDEX
(विषय सूची)

AT A GLANCE

INDEX
(विषय सूची)

AT A GLANCE

INDEX
(विषय सूची)

AT A GLANCE

INDEX
(विषय सूची)

AT A GLANCE

INDEX
(विषय सूची)

AT A GLANCE

Preface

Hindi is the most widely spoken language of the Indian subcontinent, centred principally in the States of Uttar Pradesh and Madhya Pradesh, in the north-central part of India. Hindi is the third principal international language, next only to Mandarin (chinese) and English, according to the Guinness Records. It is spoken as the first language by 225 million people throughout India, nearly 250,000 in Fiji and by many more as an immigrant language in Great Britain, South Africa, Mauritius in the Indian Ocean, in Trinidad, Guyana and Suriname. It is the *Lingua Franca* or the national language of free India.

Like most of the languages of northern India, Hindi has descended from Sanskrit. While the early literary Hindi was based on the Khari Boli ("Straight Speech") dialect, Braj Bhasa, Avadhi, Bagheli, Chattisgarhi, Bundeli and Kanauji, pure Hindi in the modern speech derives most of its vocabulary from Sanskrit. The original variety was known as the Hindustani, spoken in New Delhi and its neghbourhood area.

Hindi has a much simpler inflectional system than does Sanskrit, although the literary language uses a great number of Sanskrit forms. Nouns and pronouns have lost the full declension in eight cases of Sanskrit and instead make use of post-positions-small words attached to the end of nouns and functioning much like English prepositions.

There are only two genders, masculine and feminine, where as Gujarati and Marathi retain three. Verbs also are much reduced in inflectional complexity with only the present and future indicative forms fully conjugated other constructions are based on participal forms.

This self-tutor of Hindi is the first attempt in a popular way to make Hindi accessable to the foreign tourist. It is a step-by-step comprehensive guide to gain command of the spoken language of Hindi. It is the result of extensive travel and research. It should serve as a useful teach-yourself-guide to India's lingua franca for anyone who has an earnest desire to learn.

– Author

I DEVNĀGARĪ ALPHABET : वर्णमाला

AT A GLANCE

Vowels : स्वर

(a) Pronunciation of vowels — स्वर उच्चारण

(b) Vowel Signs — स्वर चिह्न

(c) Three more signs — तीन अन्य चिह्न

Consonants व्यंजन

(a) Pronunciation of consonants — व्यंजनों के उच्चारण

(b) About Consonants — व्यंजनों के संबंध में

(c) Addition of Vowel signs to consonants — मात्रायुक्त व्यंजन

(d) Nasals — अनुनासिक

(e) Conjunct Consonants — संयुक्ताक्षर

(f) Rules of Pronunciation — उच्चारण की विधि

(g) 'र्' or र in combination — र् या र का संयोग

Vowels : स्वर

Pronuciation of Vowels : स्वर उच्चारण

There are 11 vowels. They are pronounced as under :-

LETTER		*PRONOUNCED* *AS*	*IN* *English*	*Hindi*
अ	a	'a'	annex	अमर
आ	ā	'ā'	father	आदर
इ	i	'i'	pin	इनकार
ई	ī	'ee'	meet	ईश
उ	u	'u'	put	अमर
ऊ	ū	'oo'	moon	ऊपर
ऋ		'ri'	grip	ऋतु
ए	e	'e'	they	वे
ऐ	ai	'ai'	aisle	ऐनक
ओ	o	'o'	go	गो
औ	au	'ow'	cow	गौ

Vowel Signs : स्वर चिह्न

अ	आ	इ	ई	उ	ऊ
	ा	ि	ी	ु	ू
ऋ	ए	ऐ	ओ	औ	
ृ	े	ै	ो	ौ	

Three More Signs : तीन अन्य चिह्न

There are three more signs which follow vowels

ं ँ :

The sign ं is called Anusvār अनुस्वार (ं)

The sign ँ is called Chandr'-bindu चन्द्र बिन्दु (ँ)

The sign : is called Visarg' विसर्ग (:)

The Anusvār (अनुस्वार) ं and the Chandr'bindu (चन्द्र बिन्दु) ँ are placed on the top of the letter. The Visarg' (विसर्ग) : is placed in the right side of the letter.

Consonants : व्यंजन

There are 33 consonants-

क्	ख्	ग्	घ्	ङ्	कवर्ग	=	क - class
k	kh	G	Gh				
च्	छ्	ज्	झ्	ञ्	चवर्ग	=	च - class
Ch	Chh	j	jh				
ट्	ठ्	ड्	ढ्	ण्	टवर्ग	=	ट - class
ṭ	ṭh	ḍ	ḍh	ṇ			
त्	थ्	द्	ध्	न्	तवर्ग	=	त - class
t	th	d	dh	n			
प्	फ्	ब्	भ्	म्	पवर्ग	=	प - class
p	ph	b	bh	ṃ			
य्	र्	ल्	व्		अन्तस्थ	=	य - class
y	r	l	v				
श्	ष्	स्	ह्		उष्म	=	श - class
ś	ṣ	s	h				

The *nether* stroke ् (्) indicates that the consonant in question is without a vovel and, when there is a vowel then only it is possible to pronounce the consonant in full.

In the following 33 consonants, the vowel अ (a) is inherent in every consonant and sounded after every one which has not the *nether* stroke.

क	ख	ग	घ	ङ	Guttural	: Those pronounced from the throat.
ka	kha	ga	gha	ṅa		
च	छ	ज	झ	ञ	Palatal	: Those pronounced from the Palate.
cha	chha	ja	jha	a		
ट	ठ	ड	ढ	ण	Cerebral	: Those pronounced from the roof of the mouth.
ṭa	ṭha	ḍa	ḍha	ṇa		
त	थ	द	ध	न	Dental	: Those pronounced from the teeth.
ta	tha	da	dha	na		
प	फ	ब	भ	म	Labial	: Those pronounced from the lips.
pa	pha	ba	bha	ma		
य	र	ल	व		Semi-Vowels	
ya	ra	la	va			
श	ष	स			Sibilants	
sa	ṣa	sa				
ह					Aspirate	
ha						

Pronunciation of Consonants : व्यंजनों के उच्चारण

Letter		Pronounced as in English-	Hindi-
क्	k	kit, kith, kin	कब, कल, कम, कमल
ख्	kh	aspirate'k '- inkhorn	खाट, खग, खड़क
ग्	g	gum, gun	गप, गज, गगन
घ्	gh	aspirate 'G' ghost	घर, घट, घन
ङ्		single, ba k	गंग, अंग, रंग-रङ्ग, गङ्ग, अङ्ग
च्	ch	church, much, such	चल, चटक, चमक, कच
छ्	chh	aspirate 'ch' Churchhill, catchhim	छत्त, छल, छः
ज्	j	jug, jar, June	जग, गज, जल
झ्	jh	aspirate 'j' as in 'hejhog' (hedgehog)	झलक, झटपट
ञ्		lu ch, bu ch, hu ch	मंच-मञ्च, कंज-कञ्ज, चंचल-चञ्चल
ट्	ṭ	tail, met, set, tub	टसर, टकटक, टकसाल
ठ्	ṭh	aspirate 'ṭ' anthill	ठग, ठठरी, ठनक
ड्	ḍ	dug, dog, dull	डकार, डगर, डर, डमरू
ढ्	ḍh	aspirate 'ḍ' redhaired	ढब, ढमढम, ढरकी, ढोल

ण्	ṇ	aṇd, graṇd, saṇd	अंड–अण्ड, कंठ–कण्ठ, कंटक–कण्टक
त्	t	like t in French or Italian	तगर, तक, तकली, तपन, तप
थ्	th	aspirated t as in <u>th</u>anks	थन, थर, थलचर
द	d	like d in French and Italian	दरदर, दरी, दही, दहन
ध	dh	aspirate d as dh in a<u>dh</u>ere	धनद, धन, धवल, धसक
न	n	name, cane, nut	नयन, नट, नग, नगद
प	p	pus, purple, pump	पद, पचपन, पचन, पवन
फ	ph	phase, phone, photo	फन, फल, फसल
ब	b	burn, bus, buzz, but	बक, बकबक, बगर, बचत
भ्	bh	aspirate b, a<u>bh</u>ore	भग, भजन, भट, भमक
म्	m	mud, much, mug	मग, मख, मकर, मगर
य्	y	young, yard, you, yet	यम, यमज, यमक
र्	r	rug, rum, run, rush	रण, रग, रजक, रथ, रज
ल्	l	lunch, lust, lush, lull	लचक, लचर, लटकन
व्	v	vulcan, vulture, virtue	वन, वचन, वर, वहम
श्	ś	shut, shuffle, shunt	शठ, शत, शर, शम
ष्	ṣ	poṣṭ, ruṣṭ, muṣṭ	षट्, षट्पद, षड्रस
स्	s	sun, son, suffer	सब, सच, सतत, सबक
ह्	h	hut, hush, hurt, hurry	हठ, हत, हर, हम

About Consonants : व्यंजनों के संबंध में

The letters क, ख, ग, ज, ड, ढ, and फ are sometimes dotted below to express a certain variation in their sounds. फ़ and ज़ resemble the sounds of F and Z respectively. ड़ and ढ़ are pronounced as ' h́ (ghorhā घोड़ा = horse) and ' hh' (parhhnā पढ़ना = to read) respectively. The pronunciation of the rest क़ (ḳ), ख़ (ḳh), ग़ (g) as in क़लम (ḳalaḿ = pen), ख़बर (ḳhabar = news), and काग़ज़ (kāgaj = paper) repectively is best learnt from any Hindi-knowing person. However, it will not matter much if they are pronounced as if there were no dots.

Addition of Vowel signs to Consonants : मात्रायुक्त व्यंजन

The vowel other than अ (a), when not at beginning of syllable, assume the following contracted shapes :-

क् + आ = क् + ा = का kā काम (kāḿ = work), मकान (makāń = house).
क् + इ = क् + ि = कि ki कि (ki = that), किरण (kiraṇ = beam),
क् + ई = क् + ी = कील kīl कील (kīl = nail).
क् + उ = क् + ु = कु Ku कुल (kul=family).
क् + ऊ = क् + ू = कू Kū कूच (kūch́ = march)
क् + ऋ = क् + ृ = कृ K कृश (k ś = lean)
क् + ए = क् + े = के ke केश (keś = hairs)

क् + ऐ = क् + ै	=	कै	kai	कैथ	(kaitĥ = the wood appler.)
क् + ओ = क् + ो	=	को	ko	कोण	(koṇ' = corner)
क् + औ = क् + ौ	=	कौ	kau	कौन	(kauń = who).

Addition of the other three signs.

क् + अं = क् + ं	=	कं	ka	कंज	(ka j' = Lotus)
क् + अँ = क् + ँ	=	कँ	kan̐	कँवल	(kanval = Lotus).
क् + अः = क + :	=	कः	kah:	कः	(kah:= who).

च	चा	चि	ची	चु	चू	चृ
cha	chā	chi	chī	chu	chū	chri
चे	चै	चो	चौ	चं	चँ	चः
che	chai	cho	chau	cham	chan̐	chah:

Vowel signs in Hindi are very regular, and the foregoing examples will apply to all other letters. The only exceptions are रु 'ru and रू 'rū' where the ु and ू signs are added in the middle of the letter.

Nasals : अनुनासिक

There are two half nasal sounds in Hindi, which are represented by the sign ं and ँ placed on the top of a letter. In pronouncing these half nasal sounds care must be taken not to close the mouth while the sound is in the process of being pronounced, lest it should become a full nasal sound, e.g., रंग (ra ǵ = colour); कहाँ (kahān̐ = where).

If the letter that follows a nasalized letter belongs to क - class, च - class, ट - class, त - class or प - class, the nasal is pronounced like the last letter (i.e. ङ्, ञ्, ण्, न्, or म्,) of its class, and represented only by a dot ं, if not the last nasal letter of its group will be with nether stroke or join with the following letter; e.g.,

रंक – रङ्क or रङ्क (poor) मंच – मञ्च or मञच (stage); दंड – दण्ड or दण्ड (punishment) गंध – गन्ध or गन्ध (smell); दंभ– दम्भ or दम्भ (pride).

If the letter that follows a nasalized letter is य, र, ल, व, श, ष, स or ह the nasal is represented only by a dot ं; e.g., संयम (saṅyaṁ), संहार (sa hār), संशय (sa śay).

If a letter that follows a nasalized letter and the nasal is pronounced from the upper part of the nose, it is represented only by ँ; e.g., पाँच (pā ch = five); बाँध (bān̐dh́ = bridge); माँग (mān̐g' = demand); गाँव (gān̐v' = village).

If a letter does not follow a nasalized letter , the nasal is pronounced from the upper part of the nose and represented only by a ँ; e.g., यहाँ (Yahān̐/here); वहाँ (vahān̐/there), हूँ (hūn̐/am); मैं (main̐=I); में (men̐=in).

That half nasal sign ँ does not give any particular indication of the last nasal letter of a group.

In case a dot ं (anusvār) is used, instead of ँ, it will create confusion; e.g., हंस (hanś = a swan) (here न् is pronounced); हँसी (han̐sī = laugh) (here न् is not pronounced).

Conjunct Consonants : संयुक्ताक्षर

A Conjunct Consonant is a combination of two or more consonants. In combining two consonants the first consonant is written and pronounced half, while the second is written and pronounced fully.

Where a combination of more than two letters occurs, the last consonant is written and pronounced in full while all the preceding letters are written and pronounced only half.

Rules for Pronunciation : उच्चारण की विधि

A word ending in a simple consonant is pronounced with its अ more or less silent, e.g., मन and फल should be pronounced as मन् and फल् it is represented by sign ' in transliteration, e.g., mań and phaĺ.

In a word of three letters ending with a vowel other than अ, the second letter, if it be a simple consonant, is pronounced with the अ silent, and represented by sign ' in transliteration, e.g., कमरा : represented as "Kamŕā" ; pronounced as 'Kamrā'.

If in a word of three letters the last two letters are simple consonants, then the final letter is pronounced half, e.g, पलक —palaḱ; इधर — idhar' ; बालक — bālaḱ.

If all the letters in a word of four letters are simple consonants, then the second and the fourth are pronounced half, e.g., गड़बड़ — garh́barh́ ; झटपट — jhat́pat́, etc.

र् or र in Combination.: र् या र – संयोग में

The letter 'र्' when forming the first consonant of a combination, is written thus ' ॅ ' on the top of the second consonant, e.g., र्+म = र्म (धर्म, कर्म) ; र्+ च = र्च, etc.

'र्' when forming the second consonant of the combination is written below the first consonant and its symbol is ' ‸ ' when combined with ट, ठ, ड and ढ, e.g., ट्+ र = ट्र, ड्+ र = ड्र; and in all other cases, mere downward stroke, e.g., प्+ र = प्र, ह्+ र = ह्र, ब्+ र = ब्र, etc.

II

REFERENCE : संदर्भ

Cardinal Numbers	अंक
Ordinal Numbers	क्रमवाचक संख्याएं
Measures of length	लम्बाई के परिमाण
Measures of Weight	तोल के परिमाण
Measures of Capacity	आयतन के परिमाण
Seven days of the week	सप्ताह के सात दिन
Twelve solar months of the year	वर्ष के बारह सौर मास
Twelve lunar months of the year	वर्ष के बारह चान्द्र मास
Six seasons of the year	वर्ष की छह ऋतुएं

AT A GLANCE

Cardinal Numbers : अंक

1.	One	वन	१	Eḱ	एक
2.	Two	टू	२	Do	दो
3.	Three	थ्री	३	Teen	तीन
4.	Four	फोर	४	Chār	चार
5.	Five	फाइव्ह	५	Pā̐nch́	पाँच
6.	Six	सिक्स्	६	Chhah́	छ:
7.	Seven	सेवन्	७	Sāt	सात
8.	Eight	एट्	८	Āth́	आठ
9.	Nine	नाइन्	९	Nau	नौ
10.	Ten	टेन्	१०	Daś	दस
11.	Eleven	इलेवन्	११	Gyārah́	ग्यारह
12.	Twelve	ट्वेल्व्	१२	Bārah́	बारह
13.	Thirteen	थॅटीन	१३	Terah́	तेरह
14.	Fourteen	फॉर्टीन्	१४	Chaudah́	चौदह
15.	Fifteen	फिफ्टीन्	१५	Pandrah́	पंद्रह
16.	Sixteen	सिक्स्टीन्	१६	Solah́	सोलह
17.	Seventeen	सेवन्टीन्	१७	Satrah́	सत्रह
18.	Eighteen	एटीन्	१८	Athārah́	अठारह
19.	Nineteen	नाइनटीन्	१९	Unnīś	उन्नीस
20.	Twenty	ट्वेंटी	२०	Bīś	बीस
21.	Twenty one	ट्वेंटी वन	२१	Ekkīś	इक्कीस
22.	Twenty two	ट्वेंटी टू	२२	Bā-ī-ś	बाईस
23.	Twenty three	ट्वेन्टी थ्री	२३	Te-ī-ś	तेईस

24.	Twenty four	ट्वेंटि फोर	२४	Chaubīś	चौबीस
25.	Twenty five	ट्वेंटि फाइव	२५	Pach-chīś	पच्चीस
26.	Twenty six	ट्वेंटि सिक्स	२६	Chhab-bīś	छब्बीस
27.	Twenty seven	ट्वेंटि सेवन	२७	Sattā-ī-ś	सत्ताईस
28.	Twenty eight	ट्वेंटि एट्	२८	Aṭṭhā-ī-ś	अट्ठाईस
29.	Twenty nine	ट्वेंटी नाइन्	२९	Untiś	उन्तीस
30.	Thirty	थर्टी	३०	Tīś	तीस
31.	Thirty one	थर्टी वन्	३१	Ektiś	इकतीस
32.	Thirty two	थर्टी टू	३२	Battiś	बत्तीस
33.	Thirty three	थर्टी थ्री	३३	Tentīś	तेंतीस
34.	Thirty four	थर्टी फोर	३४	Chauntīś	चौंतीस
35.	Thirty five	थर्टी फाइव्	३५	Paintiś	पैंतीस
36.	Thirty six	थर्टी सिक्स्	३६	Chhatiś	छत्तीस
37.	Thirty seven	थर्टी सेवन्	३७	Saintīś	सैंतीस
38.	Thirty eight	थर्टी एट्	३८	Aḍtiś	अड़तीस
39.	Thirty nine	थॅर्टी नाइन्	३९	Untāliś	उनतालीस
40.	Forty	फॅार्टी	४०	Chāliś	चालीस
41.	Forty one	फॅार्टी वन्	४१	Ektālīś	इक्तालीस
42.	Forty two	फॅार्टी टू	४२	Bayālīś	बयालीस
43.	Forty three	फॅार्टी थ्री	४३	Taintālīś	तेंतालीस
44.	Forty four	फॅार्टी फोर	४४	Chauvālīś	चौवालीस
45.	Forty five	फॅार्टी फाइव्	४५	Paintālīś	पैंतालीस
46.	Forty six	फॅार्टी सिक्स्	४६	Chhiyālīś	छियालीस
47.	Forty seven	फॅार्टी सेवन्	४७	Saintālīś	सैंतालीस

48.	Forty eight	फॉर्टी एट	४८	A hatālīś	अड़तालीस
49.	Forty nine	फॉटी नाइन´	४९	Unchāś	उनचास
50.	Fifty	फ़िफ़्टि	५०	Pachāś	पचास
51.	Fifty one	फ़िफ़्टि वन	५१	Ikyāvan	इक्यावन
52.	Fifty two	फ़िफ़्टि टू	५२	Bāvan	बावन
53.	Fifty three	फ़िफ़्टि थ्री	५३	Tir'pan	तिरपन
54.	Fifty four	फ़िफ़्टि फॉं	५४	Chauvan	चौवन
55.	Fifty five	फ़िफ़्टि फाइव	५५	Pach'pań	पचपन
56.	Fifty six	फ़िफ़्टि सिक्स	५६	Chhappan	छप्पन
57.	Fifty seven	फ़िफ़्टि सेवन	५७	Sattāvań	सत्तावन
58.	Fifty eight	फ़िफ़्टि एट	५८	Aṭ-ṭhāvań	अट्ठावन
59.	Fifty nine	फ़िफ़्टि नाइन´	५९	Unsaṭh'	उनसठ
60.	Sixty	सिक्स्टि	६०	Sāṭh'	साठ
61.	Sixty one	सिक्स्टि वन	६१	Ek'saṭh'	इकसठ
62.	Sixty two	सिक्स्टि टू	६२	Bāsaṭh'	बासठ
63.	Sixty three	सिक्स्टि थ्री	६३	Tir'saṭh	तिरसठ
64.	Sixty four	सिक्स्टि फोर	६४	Chaunsaṭh'	चौंसठ
65.	Sixty five	सिक्स्टि फाइव	६५	Painsaṭh'	पैंसठ
66.	Sixty six	सिक्स्टि सिक्स	६६	Chiyāsaṭh'	छियासठ
67.	Sixty seven	सिक्स्टि सेवन	६७	Saḍ saṭh'	सड़सठ
68.	Sixty eight	सिक्स्टि एट	६८	A h' saṭh'	अड़सठ
69.	Sixty nine	सिक्स्टि नाइन´	६९	Unhattar	उनहत्तर
70.	Seventy	सेवन्टि	७०	Sattar	सत्तर
71.	Seventy one	सेवन्टी वन	७१	Ek'hattar	इकहत्तर

72. Seventy two	सेवन्टी टू	७२	Bahattar	बहत्तर
73. Seventy three	सेवन्टी थ्री	७३	Tihattar	तिहत्तर
74. Seventy four	सेवन्टी फॉ	७४	Chauhattar	चौहत्तर
75. Seventy five	सेवन्टी फाइव	७५	Pachhattar	पचहत्तर
76. Seventy six	सेवन्टी सिक्स	७६	Chhihattar	छिहत्तर
77. Seventy seven	सेवन्टी सेवन	७७	Sat´hattar	सतहत्तर
78. Seventy eight	सेवन्टी एट	७८	Aṭhattar	अठहत्तर
79. Seventy nine	सेवन्टी नाइन	७९	Unāsī	उनासी
80. Eighty	एटी	८०	Assī	अस्सी
81. Eighty one	एटी वन	८१	Ekyāsī	इक्यासी
82. Eighty two	एटी टू	८२	Bayāsī	बयासी
83. Eighty three	एटी थ्री	८३	Tirāsī	तिरासी
84. Eighty four	एटी फॉ	८४	Chaurāsī	चौरासी
85. Eighty five	एटी फाइव	८५	Pachāsī	पचासी
86. Eighty six	एटी सिक्स	८६	Chhiyāsī	छियासी
87. Eighty seven	एटी सेवन	८७	Satāsī	सतासी
88. Eighty eight	एटी एट	८८	Aṭhāsī	अठासी
89. Eighty nine	एटी नाइन´	८९	Navāsī	नवासी
90. Ninety	नाइन्´टी	९०	Nabbe	नब्बे
91. Ninety one	नाइन्´टी वन	९१	Ekyāna be	इक्यानबे
92. Ninety two	नाइन्´टी टू	९२	Bāna be	बानबे
93. Ninety three	नाइन्´टी थ्री	९३	Tirāna be	तिरानबे
94. Ninety four	नाइन्´टी फॉ	९४	Chaurānabe	चौरानबे
95. Ninety five	नाइन्´टी फाइव	९५	Pachāna be	पंचानबे

96. Ninety six	नाइन्´टी सिक्स्	९६	Chiyān be	छियानब
97. Ninety seven	नाइन्´टी सेवन्	९७	Satan be	सत्तानबे
98. Ninety eight	नाइन्´टी एट्	९८	Aṭhāńbe	अट्ठानबे
99. Ninety nine	नाइन्´टी नाइन्´	९९	Ninyān be	निन्यानबे
100. One hundred	वन´ हड्रेड्	१००	Eḱ sau	एक सौ
			(sau)	(सौ)
101. One hundred	वन्´ हड्रेड्	१०१	Eḱsau	एक सौ
and one	ऑण्ड वन		eḱ	एक
199. One hundred	वन्´हंड्रेड्	१९९	Eḱ sau	एक सौ
ninety nine	नाइन्´टी नाइन्´		ninyān be	निन्यानबे
200. Two hundred	टू हड्रेड्	२००	Do sau	दो सौ
500. Five hundred	फाइव्´हड्रेड्	५००	Pā cḣ sau	पांच सौ
1000. One	वन्´	१०००	Eḱ hazār	एक हज़ार
thousand	थाउज़ण्ड्			
1987. One	वन्´	१९८७	Eḱ	एक
thousand	थाउज़ंड		hazãr	हज़ार
nine hundred	नाइन्´ हड्रेड्		nau sau	नौ सौ
eighty seven,	एटीं सेवन्,		satãsī, yā	सतासी
or Ninteen	ऑ, नाइन्´टीन		unnīś	या उन्नीस
hundred	हड्रेड्		sau	सौ
eighty seven	एटी-सेवन		satāsī	सतासी
10,000. Ten	टेन्	१०.०००	Daś	दस
thousand	थाउज़ंड्		hazār	हज़ार

1,00.000	One	वन्'	१,००,०००	Eḱ lākh́	एक लाख
	hundred	हन्ड्रेड			
	thousand	थाउज़ंड्			
	or	ऑ,			
	A lac	अ लॅक्			
10.00.000	One	वन्'	१०.००.०००	Daś	दस
		million,		मिलिऑन्	
lākh́	लाख				
or	Ten	ऑ, टेन्			
	lac,	लॅक			
1.00,00,000	Ten	टेन्	१.००,००.०००	Ek′	एक
	million	मिलिऑन		karo h	करोड़
10,00,00,000	Hundred	हन्ड्रेड	१०,००,००,०००	Das	दस
	Million	मिलिऑन		karo h	करोड
1,00.00.00,000	One	वन्'	१,००.००.००,०००	Ek′	एक
	Billion	बिलिऑन्		arab′	अरब

Ordinal Numbers : क्रमवाचक संख्या

First	फर्स्ट्	Pahílā, Pahilā	पहला, पहिला
Second	सेकंड्	Dūśrā	दूसरा
Third	थर्ड्	Tīśrā	तीसरा
Fourth	फोर्थ्	Chauthā	चौथा
Fifth	फिफ्थ्	Pānchv́ān̐	पाँचवाँ
Sixth	सिक्स्थ्	Cha ṭhā	छठा
Seventh	सेवन्थ्	Sātvān̐	सातवाँ
Eighth	एट्थ्	Āṭhv́ān̐	आठवाँ
Ninth	नाइन्थ्	Nauv́ān̐	नौवाँ

Tenth	टेन्थ्	Daśvān̐	दसवाँ
Eleventh	एलेवन्थ्	Gyārahvān̐	ग्यारहवाँ
Twelfth	ट्वेल्फ्थ्	Barahvān̐	बारहवाँ
Thirteenth	थर्टीन्थ्	Terahvān̐	तेरहवाँ
Fourteenth	फोर्टीन्थ्	Chaudahvān̐	चौदहवाँ
Fifteenth	फिफ्टीन्थ्	Pa d rahvān̐	पन्द्रहवाँ
Twentieth	ट्वेन्टीएथ्	Bīśvān̐	बीसवाँ
Thirtieth	थर्टी एथ्	Tīśvān̐	तीसवाँ
Fiftieth	फिफ्टी एथ्	Pachās vān	पचासवाँ
Sixty-first	सिक्स्टी-फर्स्ट्	Ek sathvān̐	इकसठवाँ
Seventy-second	सेवन्टी-सेकंड्	Bahattar vān	बहतरवाँ
Hundredth	हं ड्रे ड् थ्	Sauvān̐	सौवाँ

1. She is the first in the class. वह वर्ग में पहली है।
   शी इज़् द फर्स्ट् इन द क्लास्। Vah varg men̐ pahlī hai.

2. Read the fifteenth lesson पन्द्रहवाँ पाठ पढ़ो।
   रीड् द फिफ्टीन्थ् लेसन्। Pandrahvān̐ pāṭh pa hho.

3. The hundredth applicant was selected सौवाँ प्रार्थी (उम्मीदवार) चुना गया।
   दहंड्रेड्थ् अप्लिकॉण्ट् वाज़् सेलेक्टेड्। Sauvān prārthī (Ummīdvār) chunā gayā.

4. I have read the first five books. मैंने पहली पाँच पुस्तकें पढ़ी हैं।
   आय् हैव्ह रेड् द फर्स्ट् फाइव्ह् बुक्स्। Mainne pahlī pānch pustaken̐ parhhī hain̐.

Measures of length : लम्बाई – परिमाण

10 Millimetres	१० मिलिमीटर्स	=	1 Centimetre	१ सेंटिमीटर
10 Centimetres	१० सेंटिमीटर्स	=	1 Decimetre	१ डेसिमीटर
10 Decimetres	१० डेसिमीटर्स	=	1 Metre	१ मीटर

(1m. = 100 cm. = 1000 m.m) = (१ एम् = १०० सी०एम्० = १००० एम्०एम्०)

10 Metres	१० मीटर्स	=	1 Decametre	१ डिकामीटर
10 Decametres	१० डिकामीटर्स	=	1 Hectometre	१ हेक्टॉमीटर
10 Hectometres	१० हेक्टॉमीटर्स	=	1 kilometre	१ किलोमीटर

Measures of Weight : वज़न का परिमाण

10 Millirams	१० मिलिग्राम्स्	=	1 Centigramme	१ सेंटिग्राम
10 Centigrammes	१० सेंटिग्राम्स्	=	1 Decigramme	१ डेसिग्राम
10 Decigrammes	१० डेसिग्राम्स्	=	1 gramme	१ ग्राम
	(१ जी = १००० एम०जी०)	=	(1 g. = 1000 m.g.)	
10 Grammes	१० ग्राम्स्	=	1 Decagramme	१ डेकाग्राम
10 Decagrammes	१० डेकाग्राम्स्	=	1 Hectogramme	१ हेक्टोग्राम
10 Hectogramme	१० हेक्टोग्राम्स्	=	1 Kilogrammes	१ किलोग्राम
	(१ केoजीo = १००० ग्राम्स्)	=	(1 k.g. = 1000grammes)	
10 Kilogrammes	१० किलोग्राम्स्	=	1 Myriogrammes	१ मीरियोग्राम
10 Myriogrammes	१० मिरियोग्राम्स्	=	1 Quintal	१ क्विंटल
10 Quintals	१० क्विंटल्स्	=	1 Metric tonne	१ मेट्रिक टन
	(१ टन = १००० के०जी०)	=	(1 tonne = 1000 k.g.)	

Measures of Capacity : समाई – परिमाण

10 Millilitres	१० मिलिलीटर्स	= 1 Centilitre	१ सेंटिलीटर
10 Centilitres	१० सेंटिलीटर्स	= 1 Decilitre	१ डेसिलीटर
10 Decilitres	१० डेसिलीटर्स	= 1 Litre	१ लीटर
(१ लीटर = १००० एम् एल्)		= (1 Litre = 1000 m.l.)	
10 Litres	१० लीटर्स	= 1 Decalitre	१ डिकालीटर
10 Decaletre	१० डेकालीटर्स	= 1 Hectolitre	१ हेक्टोलीटर
10 Hectolitre	१० हेक्टालीटर्स	= 1 Kilolitre	१ किलोलीटर

Seven Days of the Week : सप्ताह के सात दिन

Sunday	संडे	Ravivār	रविवार
Monday	मंडे	Somvār	सोमवार
Tuesday	टयूस्डे	Manglvār	मंगलवार
Wednesday	बेन्ज् डे	Budhvār	बुधवार
Thursday	थर्स्डे	Guruvār	गुरुवार
Friday	फ्राइडे	Shukr vār	शुक्रवार
Saturday	सटर्डे	Shanivār	शनिवार

Twelve Solar Months of the Year : वर्ष के बारह सौर मास

January	जॉन्युअरि	Janavarī	जनवरी
February	फेब्रुअरि	Far varī	फरवरी
March	मार्च्	March	मार्च

April	ॲप्रिल्	Apraiĺ	अप्रैल
May	मे	Ma-ī	मई
June	जून्	Jūn	जून्
July	जुलाइ	Julā-ī	जुलाई
August	ऑगस्ट्	Agast́	अगस्त
September	सेप्टेम्बर्	Sitambar	सितंबर
October	ऑक्टोबर्	Akṭūbar	अक्टूबर
Noveber	नॉव्हेम्बर्	Navambar	नवम्बर
December	डिसेम्बर्	Disambar	दिसंबर

Twelve Lunar Months of the Year : वर्ष के बारह चान्द्र मास

Chaiťr	चैत्र	Corresponding to March-April
Vaishākh́	वैशाख	Corresponding to April-May
Jyeṣṭh́	ज्येष्ठ	Corresponding to May-June
Āṣāḍh́	आषाढ	Corresponding to June-July
Shrāvaṇ´	श्रावण	Corresponding to July-August
Bhādr paď	भाद्रपद	Corresponding to August-September
Āshvin	आश्विन	Corresponding to September-October
Kārtiḱ	कार्तिक	Corresponding to October-November
Mārǵshīrṣ´	मार्गशीर्ष	Corresponding to November-December
Pauṣ´	पौष	Corresponding to December-Junuary
Māgh́	माघ	Corresponding to Junuary-February
Phāĺguń	फाल्गुन	Corresponding to February-March

Six Seasons of the Year : वर्ष की छ: ऋतुएँ

Seasons	ऋतुएँ	Comprising the Two Lunar Months.
सीज़न्स्	Ritu-en̐	दो चान्द्र मास अंतर्भूत
1. the Spring	वसंत	चैत्र और वैशाख
द स्प्रिंग	Vasant́	Chaitr and Vaishākh́
2. Summer	ग्रीष्म	ज्येष्ठ और आषाढ
समर्	Grīṣm	Jyeṣtḱ and Äṣāḍh́
3. Rainy Season	वर्षा	श्रावण और भाद्रपद
रेनि सीज़न्	Varṣā	Shrāvaṇ´ and Bhādrápad́
4. Autumn	शरद्	आश्विन और कार्तिक
आटम्	Sharad	Āshviń and Kārtiḱ
5. Cold Season	हेमंत	मार्गशीर्ष और पौष
कोल्ड् सीज़न	Hemant́	Mārǵshīrṣ´ and Pauṣ́
6. Winter	शिशिर	माघ और फाल्गुन
विंटर	Shishir	Māgh́ and Phālguń

III BASIC GRAMMAR
आधारभूत व्याकरण

AT A GLANCE

Formation of Sentences : वाक्य रचना

(a) Vocabulary : शब्दावली

this	दिस्	Yah́	यह
that	दैट्	vah́	वह
what	व्हाट्	kyā	क्या
where	व्हेअर	kahān̐	कहाँ
is	इज़्	hai	है
are	आर्	hain̐	हैं
and	ऍण्ड्	aur	और
also	ऑल्सो	bhī	भी
in	इन्	men̐	में
on	ऑन्	par	पर
book	बुक्	kitāb́	किताब f.
paper	पेपर्	kāgaj	कागज़ m.
ink	इंक्	syāhī	स्याही f.
pen	पेन्	kalam \u0301	कलम f.
chair	चेअर्	kursī	कुर्सी f.
table	टेबल्	mez	मेज़ f.
floor	फ्लोर्	farsh́	फर्श m.
ground	ग्राउँड्	zamīń	जमीन f.
hand	हैण्ड्	hath́	हाथ m
pencil	पेंसिल	peńsiĺ	पेंसिल f.

(b) There are only two genders in Hindi – Masculine and Feminine. Lifeless things are either masculine or feminine. Practice must determine their gender.

(c) The order of words in a Hindi sentence : the nominative with all its adjuncts comes first, next the object, and the verb last.

(d) There are no Articles in Hindi.

(e) Postpositions follow the noun and pronoun.

(f)

What is that ? व्हाट् इज़् दॅट् ?	वह क्या है ? Vaĥ kyā hai ?
That is a book दॅट् इज़् अ बुक्।	वह किताब है। Vaĥ kitāb́ hai.
Where is the pen ? व्हेअर्- इज़् द॔ पेन् ?	कलम कहाँ है ? Kalamٰ kahān̐ hai ?
The pen is in the hand. द॔ पेन् इज़् इन् द॔ हॅण्ड्।	कलम हाथ में है। kalamٰ hāth́ men̐ hai.
Where is that paper ? व्हेअर्- इज़् दॅट् पेपर् ?	वह कागज कहाँ है ? Vaĥ kāgaj kahān̐ hai ?
That paper is on the table. दॅट् पेपर् इज़् ऑन् द॔ टेबल्।	वह कागज मेज पर है। Vaĥ kāgaj mej́ par hai.
Where are the paper and the pen ?	कागज और कलम कहाँ हैं ?

व्हेअर् आर द् पेपर् अॅण्ड् द् पेन् ?	Kāgaj aur kalaṁ kahān̐ hain?
The paper and the pen are on the table	कागज और कलम मेज पर हैं।
द् पेपर अॅण्ड् द् पेन् आर् ऑन द् टेबल्	Kāgaj aur kalaṁ mej par hain̐.
Where is the chair ?	कुर्सी कहाँ है ?
व्हेअर् इज़् द् चेअर् ?	Kursī kahān̐ hai ?
Where is the book ?	किताब कहाँ है ?
व्हेअर् इज़् द् बुक् ?	Kitāb kahān̐ hai ?
The book is on the table.	किताब मेज़ पर है।
द् बुक् इज़् ऑन् द् टेबल्।	Kitāb mej par hai ?
What is on the floor ?	जमीन पर क्या है ?
व्हाट् इज़् ऑन् द् फ्लोर् ?	Jamīn par kyā hai ?
The table is on the floor.	जमीन पर मेज़ है।
द् टेबल् इज़् ऑन द् फ्लोर्।	Jamīn par mej hai.
The chair is also on the floor.	कुर्सी भी जमीन पर है।

दॅ चेअ- इज़् आलसो ऑन् दॅ फ्लोर्।	Kursī bhī jamīń par hai.
What is this ?	यह क्या है ?
व्हाट् इज़् दिस् ?	Yah kyā hai ?
This is a pencil.	यह पेंसिल है।
दिस् इज़् अ पेंसिल्।	Yah pencil hai.

To be in Present Tense : 'होना' का वर्तमान काल

Vocabulary : शब्दावली

(a) Personal Pronouns : पुरुषवाचक सर्वनाम

1.	I	आय्	Main̐	मैं
2.	Thou, you	दॉउ, यू	Tū	तू
3.	He/She/It	ही/शी/इट् (proximat)	Yah	यह
4.	He/She/It	ही/शी/इट्	Vah	वह
5.	We	वी	Ham	हम
6.	You (plural)	यू	Tum	तुम
7.	You (respect)	यू	Āp	आप
8.	They (proximate)	दे	Ye	ये
9.	They	दे	Ve	वे

(b) Masculine Nouns ending in Vowels : पुल्लिंग स्वरांत संज्ञाएँ

1.	Kisān	किसान	Farmer	फार्मर्
2.	Maźdūr	मज़दूर	labourer	लेबरर्

3.	Muni	मुनि	Ascetic	असेटिक्
4.	Dhobī	धोबी	Washerman	वाशर्रमॅन्
5.	Shatrū	शत्रु	Enemy	एनिमी
6.	Ḍākū	डाकू	Dacoit	डकैट्
7.	Rediyo	रेडियो	Radio	रेडियो

(c) Adjectives : विशेषण

1.	Santuṣṭ	संतुष्ट	Satisfied	सटिस्फाइड्
2.	Prasanna	प्रसन्न	Happy	हॅप्पी
3.	Mūrkh	मूर्ख	Foolish	फूलिश्
4.	Chatur	चतुर	Clever	क्लेव्ह
5.	Amīr	अमीर	Rich	रिच्
6.	Garīb	ग़रीब	Poor	पुअ
7.	Kharāb	खराब	Bad	बॅड्
8.	Krūr	क्रूर	Cruel	क्रुएल्
9.	Madhur	मधुर	Sweet	स्वीट्

(d) Auxiliary Verb to be : सहायक क्रिया to be (हो)

1.	Hūn̐	हूँ	Am	ॲम्
2.	Hai	है (हि)	Is	इज़्
3.	Hain	हैं (हिं)	Are	अ
4.	Ho	हो	Are	आ

Personal Pronouns : पुरुषवाचक सर्वनाम

	Singular		*Plural*	
1st person	(I)	मैं	(we)	हम
2nd person	(Thou, You)	तू	(you)	तुम
			(respectful)	आप
3rd Person	(He/She/It)	यह	(they)	ये
	(He/She/It)	वह	(they)	वे

The forms of हो (to be) shown with the respective pronoun as subject in the brackets :

	Singular			*Plural*		
1st Person	(मैं)	हूँ	(am)	(हम)	हैं	(are)
2nd Person	(तू)	है	(are, is)	(तुम)	हो	(are)
				(आप)	हैं	(are)
3rd Person	(यह)	है	(is)	(ये)	हैं	(are)
	(वह)	है	(is)	(वे)	हैं	(are)

Pronouns with the Auxiliary Verbs : सहायक क्रिया के साथ सर्वनाम

1st Person	मैं हूँ	I am	हम हैं	We are
2nd Person	तू है	You are,	तुम हो	You are
			आप हैं	You are
3rd Person	यह है	He/She/It is	ये हैं	They are
	वह है	He/She/It is	वे हैं	They are

Sentences with Nouns : संज्ञाओं के साथ वाक्य

I am a farmer	मैं किसान हूँ
आय् ॲम् अ फार्मर्	Main̐ kisāń hūn̐
We are farmers	हम किसान हैं
वी आर्- फार्मर्स्	Hamí kisāń hain̐
You are a labourer	तू मज़दूर है
यू आर्- अ लेबर्र्	Tū maźdūr hai
You are a labourer	तुम मज़दूर हो
यू आर्- अ लेबर्र्	Tumí maźdūr ho
You are an ascetic	आप मुनि हैं
यू आर्- ॲन् असेटिक्	Āṕ muni hain̐
He is a washerman	वह धोबी है
ही इज़् अ वाशर्मॅन्	Vaḿ dhobī hai
They are enemies	वे शत्रु हैं
दे आर्- एनिमीज़्	Ve shatru hain̐
He is a docoit	यह डाकू है
ही इज़् अ डकैट्	Yaḿ dāku hai
They are radioes	ये रेडियो हैं
दे आर्- रेडिओस्	Ye rediyo hain̐

Sentences with Adjectives : विशेषणों के साथ वाक्य

I am satisfied	मैं संतुष्ट हूँ
आय् ॲम् सटिस्फाइड्	Main̐ sa tuṣṭ́ hūn̐
We are happy	हम प्रसन्न हैं
वी आ– हॅप्पी	Huḿ prasanna hain̐
You are foolish	तू मूर्ख है
यू आ- फूलिश्	Tū mūrkh́ hai
You are clever	तुम चतुर हो
यू आ- क्लेव्ह-	Tuḿ chatur ho
You are rich	आप अमीर हैं
यू आ– रिच्	Āṕ amīr hain̐
He is poor	वह गरीब है
ही इज़् पुअ-	Vah́ garīb́ hai
They are bad	वे खराब हैं
दे आ– बॅड्	Ve kharāb́ hain̐
It is cruel	यह क्रूर है
इट् इज़् क्रुएल्	Yah́ krūr hai

They are sweet ये मधुर हैं
दे आर्- स्वीट् Ye madhur hain̐

Uses of हाँ, न, नहीं : हाँ, न, नहीं के प्रयोग

Masculine Nouns

1.	Ghar	घर	House	हाउस्
2.	Hāth́	हाथ	Hand	हॅण्ड्
3.	Pūl	पुल	Bridge	ब्रिज्
4.	Phūl	फूल	Flower	फ्लॉवर्
5.	Drāivar	ड्राइवर	Driver	ड्राइवर्
6.	Injiniar	इंजिनिअर	Engineer	एन्जिनिअर्

Pronouns

1.	Kaun	कौन	Who	हू
2.	Kyā	क्या	What	व्हॉट्

Adverbs

1.	Yahān̐	यहाँ	Here	हिअ-
2.	Vahān̐	वहाँ	There	देअ-
3.	Kahān̐	कहाँ	Where	व्हेअ-

Post positions

1.	Meṅ	में	In	इन्
2.	Par	पर	On, at	ऑन्, ॲट

The Post position follows the noun.

1. Who are you ?
   व्हू आर्- यू ?
   तुम कौन हो ?
   Tuṁ kaun ho ?

2. I am Rāma.
   आय् ॲम राम ।
   मैं राम हूँ।
   Maiṅ Raṁ hūṅ.

3. Where is Ramesha ?
   व्हेअ- इज़् रमेश ?
   रमेश कहाँ है ?
   Ramesh kahāṅ hai ?

4. Ramesha is in the house.
   रमेश इज़् इन् द हॉउस्.
   रमेश घर में है।
   Ramesh ghar meṅ hai.

5. What are you ?
   व्हॉट् आर्- यू ?
   तुम क्या हो ?
   Tuṁ kyā ho ?

6. I am a driver.
   आय् ॲम् अ ड्राइव्हर्.
   मैं ड्राइवर हूँ।
   Maiṅ drāivar hūṅ

7. Who is there ?
   व्हू इज़् देअ- ?
   वहाँ कौन है ?
   Vahāṅ kaun hai ?

8. There are labourers on the bridge.
देअर्- आर्- लेबरर्स ऑन् दं ब्रिज्.

वहाँ पुल पर मज़दूर हैं

Vahān̐ pul par mazdūr hain̐

9. Engineers are here.
एंजिनिअर्स आर्- हिअर्-.

इंजिनियर यहाँ हैं।

Inginiyar yahān̐ hain̐

10. What is there in the hand ?
व्हॉट् इज़् देअर्- इन् दं हॅण्ड् ?

हाथ में क्या है ?

Hath men̐ kyā hai ?

11. A flower is in the hand.
अ फ्लाव्ह्- इज़् इन् दं हॅण्ड्

हाथ में फूल है।

Hath men̐ phūl hai.

Nouns

1.	Sādhu	साधु	Saint	सेंट्
2.	Atithi	अतिथि	Guest	गेस्ट्
3.	Jauharī	जौहरी	Jeweller	ज्युवेलर्
4.	Naukar	नौकर	Servant	सर्वेंट्
5.	Sipāhī	सिपाही	Sepoy	सिपॉय्

Adverbs

1.	Hān̐	हाँ	Yes	यस्
2.	Nahīn̐	नहीं	Not	नॉट्
3.	Na	न	No	नो

Rule : Nahīṅ (नहीं) comes just before the verb.

kyā (क्या) is also used as an indeclinable word in the beginning of Interrogative Sentences.

Examples :

1. Kyā vaḣ kisāṅ hai ? क्या वह किसान है ?	Is he a farmer ? इज़् ही अ फार्मर् ?
2 Kyā tuṁ mażdūr ho ? क्या तुम मज़दूर हो ?	Are you a labourer ? आर्-यू अ लेबरर?
3. Kyā maiṅ mūrkh hūṅ ? क्या मैं मूर्ख हूँ ?	Am I foolish ? ॲम् आय् फूलिश् ?
4. Kyā ve kisāṅ haiṅ ? क्या वे किसान हैं ?	Are they farmers ? आर्- दे फार्मर्स् ?
5. Hāṅ, ve kisāṅ haiṅ. हाँ, वे किसान हैं।	Yes, they are farmers. यस्, दे आ- फार्मर्स्.
6. Kyā vaḣ jauharī hai ? क्या वह जौहरी है ?	Is he a jeweller ? इज़् ही अ ज्यूवेलर् ?
7. Na, vaḣ jauharī nahīṅ hai. न, वह जौहरी नहीं है।	No, he is not a jeweller. नो, ही इज़् नॉट् अ ज्यूवेलर्.

8. Kyā vaḣ sādhu hai ? क्या वह साधु है ?	Is he a saint ? इज़् ही अ सेंट् ?
9. Hān̐, vaḣ sādhu hai. हाँ, वह साधु है।	Yes, he is a saint. यस् ही इज़् अ सेंट्.
10. Kyā ve sipāhī hain̐ ? क्या वे सिपाही हैं ?	Are they sepoys ? आ- दे सिपाय्ज़् ?
11. Na, ve sipāhī nahīn̐ hain̐. न, वे सिपाही नहीं हैं।	No, they are not sepoys. नो, दे आ- नॉट् सिपाय्ज़्
12. Kyā ve atithi hain̐ ? क्या वे अतिथि हैं ?	Are they guests ? आ- दे गेस्ट्स् ?
13. Hān̐ ve atithi hain̐. हाँ, वे अतिथि हैं।	Yes, they are guests. यस्, दे आ- गेस्ट्स्.
14. Kyā ve naukar hain̐ ? क्या वे नौकर हैं ?	Are they servants ? आ- दे सर्व्हंट्स् ?
15. Na, ve naukar nahīn̐ hain̐. न, वे नौकर नहीं हैं।	No, they are not servants. नो, दे आ- नॉट् सर्वेंट्स्.
16. Ve shatru hain̐. वे शत्रु हैं.	They are enemies. दे आ- एनिमीज़्.

Words ending in आ (ā) : आकारान्त शब्द

Nouns ending in आ (ā)

1.	La akā	लड़का	Boy	बॉय्
2.	Gho ā	घोड़ा	Horse	हॉर्स्
3.	Shāhzādā	शाहज़ादा	Prince	प्रिंस्
4.	La vaiyā	लड़वैया	Fighter	फ़ायटर
5.	Kap ā	कपड़ा	Cloth	क्लॉथ्
6.	Bachchā	बच्चा	Baby	बेबी
7.	Ādamī	आदमी	Man	मॅन्
8.	Gadhā	गधा	Donkey	डाड.की
9.	Kuttā	कुत्ता	Dog	डॉग
10.	Mantrī	मंत्री	Minister	मिनिस्टर्

Adjectives ending in आ (ā)

1.	Achchhā	अच्छा	Good	गुड्
2.	Kālā	काला	Black	ब्लैक्
3.	Purānā	पुराना	Old	ओल्ड्
4.	Nayā	नया	New	न्यू
5.	Pyārā	प्यारा	Lovely	लवली
6.	Chhotā	छोटा	Small	स्माल्
7.	Bhūrā	भूरा	Brown	ब्राउन्

आ, ए, ई

Rule : Masculine words *i.e.* nouns, adjectives, verbs and adjectival suffix) ending in आ form their plurals by changing the final आ into ए and their feminine (singular and plural) by changing the आ into ई,

Mas. Sing.	*Mas. Plu*	*Fem.*	
लड़का	लड़के	लड़की	(noun)
अच्छा	अच्छे	अच्छी	(adjective)
जाता	जाते	जाती	(verb)
राम का	राम के	राम की	(adjectival suffix)

Kyā vah́ la kā hai ?	Is he a boy ?
क्या वह लड़का है ?	इज़् ही अ बॉय् ?
Hān, vah́ la kā hai.	Yes, he is a boy.
हाँ, वह लड़का है।	यस्, ही इज़् अ बॉय्.
Vah́ achchhā la kā hai.	He is a good boy.
वह अच्छा लड़का है।	ही इज़् अ गुड् बॉय्.
Vah́ achchhī la kī hai.	She is a good girl.
वह अच्छी लड़की है।	शी इज़् अ गुड् गर्ल्.
Kyā ve la ke hain̐?	Are they boys ?
क्या वे लड़के हैं ?	आ- दे बायज़् ?
Hān̐ ve la ke hain̐	Yes, they are boys.
हाँ, वे लड़के हैं।	यस् दे आ- बायज़्.

Ve achchhe la ke hain̐ वे अच्छे लड़के हैं।	They are good boys. दे आ॑ गुड् बाय्ज़्.
Kyā vaḿ gho ā hai? क्या वह घोड़ा है ?	Is he a horse ? इज़् ही अ हॉर्स् ?
Hān̐ vaḿ gho ā hai. हाँ, वह घोड़ा है।	Yes, he is a horse. यस् ही इज़् अ हॉर्स्.
Vaḿ kālā gho ā hai. वह काला घोड़ा है।	He is a black horse. ही इज़् अ ब्लैक् हॉर्स्.
Kyā ve gho e hain̐ ? क्या वे घोड़े हैं ? Hān̐, ve gho e hain̐. हाँ, वे घोड़े हैं।	Are they horses ? आ॑ दे हॉर्सेस् ? Yes, they are horses. यस्, दे आ- हॉर्सेस्.
Ve gho e bhūre hain̐. वे घोड़े भूरे हैं।	They are brown horses. दे आ- ब्राउन् हॉर्सेस्.
Kyā āṕ shāh́jada hain̐ ? क्या आप शाहज़ादा हैं ?	Are you a prince ? आ- यू अ प्रिन्स् ?
Hān̐ main̐ shāh́jādā hūn̐. हाँ, मैं शाहज़ादा हूँ।	Yes, I am a prince. यस्, आय् ॲम् अ प्रिन्स्.

Kyā ve shaȟjāde hain̐ ?
क्या वे शाहज़ादे हैं ?

Are they princes ?
आर्- दे प्रिन्सेस् ?

Na, ve shaȟjāde nahīn̐ hain̐.
न, वे शाहज़ादे नहीं हैं।

No, they are not princes.
नो, दे आर्- नॉट् प्रिन्सेस्.

Ve la vaiye hain̐.
वे लड़वैये हैं।

They are fighters.
दे आर्- फायटर्स्.

Kyā kapa e purāne hain̐ ?
क्या कपड़े पुराने हैं ?

Are the clothes old ?
आर् द क्लोद्स् ओल्ड् ?

No, kapa e purāne nahīn̐ hain̐.
न, कपड़े पुराने नहीं हैं।

No, the clothes are not old.
नो, द क्लोद्स् आर्- नॉट् ओल्ड् .

Kapa e naye hain̐.
कपड़े नए हैं।

The clothes are new.
द क्लोद्स् आर्- न्यू.

Ve kaun hain̐ ?
वे कौन हैं ?

Who are they ?
व्हू आर्- दे ?

Ve bachche hain̐.
वे बच्चे हैं।

They are children.
दे आर्- चिल्ड्रन्.

Ve pyāre bachche hain̐. वे प्यारे बच्चे हैं।	They are lovely children. दे आर्- लव्ली चिल्ड्रन्.
Ye chhoṭe kutte hain̐. ये छोटे कुत्ते हैं।	They are small dogs. दे आर्- स्माल् डॉग्स्.
Kyā vah ādmī hai ? क्या वह आदमी है ?	Is he a man ? इज़् ही अ मॅन् ?
Na, vah ādmī nahīn̐ hai. न, वह आदमी नहीं है।	No, he is not a man. नो, ही इज़् नॉट् अ मॅन्.
Vah gadhā hai. वह गधा है।	He is a donkey. ही इज़् अ डॉङ्की.

Past & Future of to be : होना का भूत और भविष्यकाल

Auxiliary verb gks (in past and future)

Masculine Sing.	thā	था	was	वाज़्
Masculine Plural	the	थे	were	वेर्अ
Feminine Sing.	thī	थी	was	वाज़्
Feminine Plural	thīn̐	थीं	were	वेर्अ
Mas S.	hogā	होगा	will be	विल् बी
Mas. P.	hoge	होगे	will be	विल् बी
Mas. P.	hon̐ge	होंगे	will be	विल् बी

Mas s. (F.P.)	hū̃gā	हूँगा	shall be	शल् बी
Fem. S.	hogī	होगी	will be	विल् बी
Fem. P.	hõgī	होंगी	will be	विल् बी
Fem. S. (F.P.)	hū̃gī	हूँगी	shall be	शल् बी

Mai̐ achchhā la akā hū̃ मैं अच्छा लड़का हूँ।	I am a good boy. आय् ॲम् अ गुड् बॉय्.
Ham achchhe la ake hai̐ हम अच्छे लड़के हैं।	We are good boys. वी आर् गुड् बायज़्.
Mai̐ achchhī la akī hū̃. मैं अच्छी लड़की हूँ।	I am a good girl. आय् ॲम् अ गुड् गर्ल्.
Vah achchhā la akā thā. वह अच्छा लड़का था।	He was a good boy. ही वाज़् अ गुड् बाय्.
Ve achchhe la ake the वे अच्छे लडके थे।	They were good boys. दे वेअ- गुड् बायज़्.
Vah achchhī la akī thī. वह अच्छी लड़की थी।	She was a good girl. शी वाज़् अ गुड् गर्ल्.
Tū/vah mantrī hogā.	You (s.)/he will be a minister.

तू/वह मंत्री होगा।	यू(शी)/ही विल् बी मिनिस्टर्.
Tuḿ mantrī hoge.	You will be minister.
तुम मंत्री होगे।	यू विल् बी मिनिस्टर्.
Āṕ/v́e/haḿ mantrī hon̐ge.	You/they/we will/shall be ministers.
आप/वि/हम मंत्री होंगे।	यू / दे /वी विल्/शल् बी मिनिस्टर्स.
Main̐ mantrī hūngā.	I shall be a minister.
मैं मंत्री हूँगा।	आय् शल् बी अ मिनिस्टर्.
Tū/vaḣ mantrī hogī.	You/she will be a minister.
तू/वह मंत्री होगी।	यू/शी विल् बी अ मिनिस्टर्.
Āṕ/ve/haḿ mantrī hon̐gī.	You/they/we (fem.) will/shall be ministers.
आप/वि/हम मंत्री होंगी।	यू/दे/ वी विल्/ शल् बी मिनिस्टर्स्.
Main̐ mantrī hūn̐gi.	I (fem.) shall be a minister.
मैं मंत्री हूँगी।	आय् शल् बी अ मिनिस्टर्.

Cases and case-endings : कारक और विभक्तियाँ

There are eight cases (कारक - kārak) in Hindi : -

Case - endings	***विभक्तियाँ***	***Vibhaktiyān***
1. Nominative or the First Case	कर्ता (कारक)	ने
2. Accusative or the Second Case	कर्म (कारक)	को (to)
3. Instrumental or the Third Case	करण (कारक)	से (by)
4. Dative or the Fourth Case	संप्रदान (कारक)	को (to) or के लिए (for)
5. Ablative or the Fifth Case	अपादान (कारक)	से (from; than)
6. Genitive or the Sixth Case	संबंध (कारक)	का, के, की (of or 's)
7. Locative or the Seventh Case	अधिकरण (कारक)	में (in); पर (on)
8. Vocative or the Eighth Case	संबोधन (कारक)	ऐ, ओ, अरे, अजी, O

The case-ending in Hindi follow the nouns and pronouns and therefore are called 'Post-positions'.

1. Main̐-ne Raḿ ko daś ruṕye diye. मैं-ने राम को दस	I gave ten rupees to Rām. आय् गेव्ह् टेन् रुपीज़् टु राम। रुपये दिये।
2. La hakā kutte ko mār tā hai. लड़का कुत्ते को मारता है।	The boy beats the dog. द॑ बॉय् बीट्स द॑ डॉग्।
3. Ve havā-ī jahāj se Dillī gaye. वे हवाई जहाज़ से दिल्ली गये।	They went to Delhi by plane. दे वेंट् टु डेल्हि बाय् प्लेन्।
4. Main̐-ne Rāḿ ko daś ruṕye diye. मैंने राम को दस रुपये दिये।	I gave ten rupees to Rāḿ. आय् गेव्ह् टेन् रुपीज़् टु राम।
5. Mohan ke li-e yah́ kāḿ karo. मोहन के लिए यह काम करो।	Do this work for Mohan. डू दिस् वर्क् फॉ मोहन।

6. Ā̐nkhoṅ se ā̐nsū tapakte hain̐.
आँखों से आँसू टपकते हैं।

Tears drop <u>from</u> the eyes.
टीअर्स् ड्रॉप् फ्रॉम् द आइज़्।

7. Gopāl se Rām baṛā hai.
गोपाल से राम बड़ा है।

Rām is older <u>than</u> Gopāl.
राम् इज़् ओल्डर् दॅन् गोपाल।

8. Is gā̐nv <u>kā</u> nām Madhupur hai.
इस गाँव <u>का</u> नाम मधुपुर है।

Name <u>of</u> this village is Madhupur.
नेम् ऑफ दिस् व्हिलेज् इज़् मधुपुर।

9. Is gā̐nv <u>ke</u>log dayālu hain̐.
इस गाँव <u>के</u> लोग दयालु हैं।

The people of this village are kind.
द पीपल् ऑफ् दिस् व्हिलेज् आ काइंड्।

10. Is gā̐nv <u>kī</u>nāriyā̐n lajjāvatī hain̐.
इस गाँव <u>की</u> नारियाँ लज्जावती हैं।

The ladies of this village are bashful.
द लेडिज़् ऑफ् दिस् व्हिलेज् आ बॉश्फुल्.

11. Yah Rām kā ghar hai. यह राम का घर है।	This is Rām's house. दिस् इज़् राम स् हाउस्।
12. Ve Rām ke gho he hain. वे राम के घोड़े हैं।	Those are Ram s horses. दोज़् आ रामस् हॉर्सेस्।
13. Gilāś men pānī hai. गिलास में पानी है।	Water is in the glass. वाटर् इज़् इन् द ग्लास्।
14. Pustak mej par hai. पुस्तक मेज़ पर है।	The book is on the table. द बुक् इज़् ऑन् द टेबल्।
15. Ai la hke! idhar ā-o. ऐ लड़के ! इधर आओ।	O boy ! come here. ओ बॉय् ! कम् हिअ्।

Plural of Feminine Nouns : स्त्रीलिंग संज्ञाओं के बहुवचन

Feminine nouns ending in अ and या form their plural by changing the final अ and या into एँ and या एँ respectively *e.g.*

पुस्तक book	पुस्तकें books	आँख eye	आँखें eyes.
कुतिया bitch	कुतियाएँ bitches	गुड़िया doll	गुड़ियाएँ dolls

Feminine nouns ending in इ or ई form their plural by adding याँ, *e.g.*,

तिथि date	तिथियाँ dates	जाति race	जातियाँ races
लड़की girl	लड़कियाँ girls	नदी river	नदियाँ rivers

Feminine nouns ending in other vowels (*i.e.* आ, उ, and ऊ form their plural by adding एँ or यें, *e.g.*

लता creaper	लताएँ लतायें creapers	दवा medicine	दवाएँ, दवायें medicines
वस्तु thing	वस्तुएँ, वस्तुयें things	बहू daughter-in-law	बहुएँ, बहुयें daughters-in-law

Note :-The final ई and ऊ of feminine nouns are shortened into इ and उ respectively before the plural suffix is added, *e.g.*, लड़की - लड़कियाँ ; बहू - बहुएँ

When a noun (masculine or feminine) is followed by a post postition (case-ending), its plural is formed by adding ओं irrespective of the above rules, *e.g.*, घर-घरों में; लड़का-लड़कों के ; पुस्तक-पुस्तकों से ; कमरा-कमरों में ; आँख-आँखों पर.

Note :- If a noun ends in इ or ई, यों is added instead of ओं, *e.g.*, स्त्री-स्त्रियों से ; जाति-जातियों में।

The Imperative : आज्ञार्थक

(Tū ā)	तू आ	(Tū baiṭh́)	तू बैठ
(Tuḿ āo)	तुम आओ	(Tuḿ baiṭho)	तुम बैठो
(Āṕ āiye)	आप आइये	(Āṕ baiṭhiye)	आप बैठिये

The above sentences are in the Imperative Mood. The Imperative mood is used when we command or request a person to do a thing.

(a) When (Tū) तू is the subject, the root of verb is itself used. the verb-root is itself the imperative form, *e.g.*, (Tū ā) तू आ come thou, (Tū baiṭh) तू बैठ sit thou, etc.

(b) When (tuḿ) तुम is the subject, ओ (o) is added to the root; *e.g.* (tuḿ āo̱) तुम आओ you come ; तुम करो (Tuḿ karo̱) you do, etc.,

(c) When (āṕ) आप is the subject, (iye) इये is added to the root, *e.g.*, (Āṕ āiye) आप आइये you (please) come ; (Āṕ baiṭhiye) आप बैठिये you (please) sit, etc.

The pronoun (Tū) तू is not commonly used for addressing equals and superiors. It is used to address children or menials. It is also used when addressing God or dearly loved persons. It may be translated 'Thou'.

The pronoun (Tum̐) तुम is used in addressing friends, equals or those who are younger to us.

The pronoun (Āp̐) आप is used in addressing superiors and persons whom we wish to respect.

(d) When (Tum̐) तुम is the subject, (do = give) दो ; and (lo = take) लो are the Imperative of दे and ले respectively (not देओ and लेओ) ।

(e) When (Āp̐) आप is the subject, the Imperative forms of दे, ले, कर, and पी are as under :

दे	दीजिये	(please) give
ले	लीजिये	(please) take
कर	कीजिए	(please) do
पी	पीजिये	(please) drink

Now-a-days 'करिये' is also used.

Tū	तू	Thou	दॉऊ
Tum̐	तुम	you	यू
Āp̐	आप	you (respectful)	यू
ā	आ	come	कम्
jā	जा	go	गो
khā	खा	eat	ईट्
pī	पी	drink	ड्रिंक्

pa h	पढ़	read	रीड्
likh́	लिख	write	राइट्
de	दे	give	गिव्
le	ले	take	टेक्
uṭh́	उठ	get up	गेट् अप्
baiṭh́	बैठ	sit	सिट्
rah́	रह	live, stay	लिव्, स्टे
dekh́	देख	see	सी
kar	कर	do	डू
lā	ला	bring	ब्रिंग्
kām	काम	work	वर्क्
mat́	मत	dońt (do not)	डोंण्ट्

The negative sense in the Imperative is expressed by adding (mat́) मत before or after the verb, *e.g.*,

Tuḿ mat jāo.	तुम मत जाओ	you don't go	यू डोंण्ट् गो
Āṕ mat jāiye.	आप मत जाइये	you don't go	यू डोंण्ट् गो
Jāo mat́.	जाओ मत	Don't go	डोंण्ट् गो

Sometimes न (no, not) is used in the place of मत to express the negative. It is milder in sense than मत ; *e.g.*, Āṕ vahān̐ na jāiye आप वहाँ न जाइये (please) dońt go there प्लीज़् डोंण्ट् गो देअ

Note :- नहीं nahīn̐ (no, not) is never used in the Imperative sentences.

Tuḿ āo.	(You) come.
तुम आओ।	(यू) कम्।

Kursī par baiṭho. कुर्सी पर बैठो।	Sit on the chair. सिट् ऑन् द चेअर्-।
Chāy̕ pījiye. चाय पीजिये।	(Please) drink tea. (प्लीज़्) ड्रिंक टी।
Tuṁ skūl jāo. तुम स्कूल जाओ।	(You) go to school. (यू) गो टु स्कूल।
Yah kitāb pa ho. यह किताब पढ़ो।	Read this book. रीड् दिस बुक्।
Hath men̐ kalam lo. हाथ में कलम लो।	Take a pen in the hand. टेक् अ पेन् इन् द हॅण्ड्।
Kagaź par likho. कागज पर लिखो	Write on the paper. राइट् ऑन् द पेपर्।
Tuṁ uṭho. तुम उठो।	You get up. यू गेट् अप्।
Jāo aur kursī lāo. जाओ और कुर्सी लाओ।	Go and bring the chair. गो ॲण्ड् ब्रिंग् द चेअर्-।
Zamīṅ par mat baitho. ज़मीन पर मत बैठो	Don’t sit on the ground. डों ण्ट् सिट् ऑन् द ग्राउंड्।

Dekho, zamīń par kyā hai. देखो, ज़मीन पर क्या है।	See, what is on the floor. सी, व्हाट् इज़् ऑन् द फ्लोर्।
Āp āiye. आप आइये।	(Please) you come. (प्लीज़्) यू कम्।
Kursī par baiṭhiye. कुर्सी पर बैठिये।	(Please) sit on the chair. (प्लीज़्) सिट् ऑन् द चेअर्-।
Yah pījiye. यह पीजिये।	(Please) drink this. (प्लीज़्) ड्रिंक् दिस्।
Yah kitāb ma pa hiye. यह किताब मत पढ़िये।	(Please) don't read this book (प्लीज़्) डोंण्ट् रीड् दिस् बुक।
Yah kitab pa hiye. यह किताब पढ़िये।	(Please) read this book. (प्लीज़्) रीड् दिस् बुक्।

The Infinitive : क्रियार्थक संज्ञा

The Infinitive is formed by adding ना (Nā) to the root of a verb ; *e.g.*, खा eat — खाना to eat ; देख see — देखना to see, etc.

There are two uses of the Infinitive :- (1) Imperative, and (2) Verbal Noun or Gerund.

As an Imperative, it is used with second person singular pronoun तू, तुम with a future force.

e.g., तुम यह काम मत करना	Don't do this work (in future).
वहाँ कभी मत जाना	Never go there.

As a Verbal Noun, it is used just as any masculine noun.

e.g., देर से जागना बुरा है।	It is bad to wake up late.
क्या उसका जाना ज़रूरी है ?	Is his going essential ?

The final letter ना of an Infinitive changes into ने when followed by a case-ending.

e.g. वहाँ जाने में देर मत करो।	Don't delay in going there.
वह पढ़ने के लिये यहाँ आता है।	He comes here to study.

Note :- 'के लिए' when followed by the verb आ or जा is often dropped after a Verbal Noun. e.g.

मैं खाने जाता हूँ।	I am going to eat.
वह रोज़ यहाँ पढ़ने आता है।	He comes here to read every day.

The Infinitive is a form of the verb changed for person, number or tense.

Kaĺ muzeh Bam̃bai jānā́ hai. कल मुझे बंबई जाना है।	I have to go to Bombay. tomorrow. आय् हैव् टु गो टू बॉम्बे टु–मारो।
Kaĺkattā jānā tumhāre liye achchhā nahīn̐. कलकत्ता जाना तुम्हारे लिए अच्छा नहीं।	It is not good for you to go to Calcutta. इट् इज़् नॉट् गुड् फॉर् यू टु गो टु कॅल्कटा।
Bār bār kāfī pīnā achchhā nahīn̐. बार–बार काफी पीना अच्छा नहीं।	Drinking Coffee often is not good. ड्रिंकिंग् कॉफी ऑफन् इज़् नॉट् गुड्।
Daur̆nā achchhā vyāyām̃ hai. दौड़ना अच्छा व्यायाम है।	Running is good exercise रनिंग् इज़् गुड् एक्सरसाइज़्।
Sīta boĺnā chāh̃tī hai. सीता बोलना चाहती है।	Sita wants to speak. सीता वांट्स् टु स्पीक्।

Participle : धातुसाधित

The Participle is that form of a verb which partakes of the nature of an adjective, noun or adverb.

1. The Present Paticiple (वर्तमानकालवाचक धातुसाधित) is formed by adding 'ता' or 'ता हुआ' to the root, *e.g.*,

Adj.—	सोता (या सोता हुआ) लड़का	A sleeping boy
	दौड़ते (या दौड़ते हुए) घोड़े	Running horses
	चलती (या चलती इुई) गाड़ी	A moving train
Adv.—	वह गाता (या गाता हुआ) आता है	He comes singing (along)
	वे रोते हुए गये	They went weeping
	राधा कोट पहनती हुई निकली	Rādhā came out putting on her coat
Noun—	डूबते को तिनके का सहारा	A straw is a support to a drowning person

When both the subject and the object are followed by their respective case-signs, the participle is always used in its inflected form.; *e.g.*,

मैने माधुरी को आते हुए देखा — I saw Madhurī coming

तुमने उन लोगों को कभी गाते — Have you ever heard them

हुए सुना है ? — singing ?

When the participle is followed by time the subject is always in the genitive and the following forms are used :

मेरे जाते समय — At the time of my going

उसके लिखते समय — At the time of his writing

वीणा के बोलते समय	At the time of Vīṇā's speaking
उसके गाते समय	At the time of his/her singing

2. The Past Participle (भूतकालवाचक धातुसाधित) is formed by adding आ to verbs ending in अ and ऊ, *e.g.*, पढ़ - पढ़ा; लिख - लिखा; डूब -डूबा; छू - छुआ.

'या' is added when a verb ends in any other vowel than अ and ऊ ; *e.g.*, आ - आया ; नहा - नहाया ; बो - बोया ; सो - सोया; धो - धोया, etc. In case a verb ends in ई or ऊ, the ई or ऊ is shortened before आ or या is added, *e.g.*, पी - पिया ; छू - छुआ.

The following are the only exceptions to this rule :- दे - दिया; ले - लिया ; जा - गया ; कर - किया ; हो — हुआ.

The Past Participle has the same form as the Past Tense. The difference is only in usage. *e.g.*,

राम ने भात खाया **(Past-tense)** Rāma ate rice.
कल का खाया आज हज़म हुआ **(Past-participle)**
The food eaten yesterday, got digested today.

पढ़ा - लिखा आदमी	an educated man
टाइप किया हुआ पत्र	a typed letter

Note :- 'हुआ' is generally added after the present or past participle ; *e.g.*, (1) दौड़ती हुई गाड़ी ; (2) खिला हुआ फूल ; (3) रमता योगी ; (4) बहता पानी ; (5) टूटी हुई कुर्सी ; (6) फटे हुए कपड़े ;

(1) moving train ; (2) blossomed flower ; (3) moving about (wandering) ascetic ; (4) flowing water; (5) broken chair; (6) torn clothes.

The Perfect Participle (पूर्णकालवाचक धातुसाधित) is formed adding 'कर' to the root, *e.g.*, खा – खाकर having eaten ; सुन – सुनकर having heard ; सो – सोकर having slept ; देख – देखकर having seen; etc.

When the participle of a transitive verb is followed by आ or जा, कर is sometimes dropped, *e.g.*,

देख आओ	See and come
सुन जाओ	Go having heard, hear and go.
देख आइये	(Please) see and come.
कर गया	Did and went

The Perfect Paticiple of कर is 'करके' (having done), and not कर कर.

Aorist Tense : प्रश्नानुमतीच्छादि–दर्शककाल

The Aorist tense, to denote purpose, condition, wish, permission interrogation, advice about an action is formed by adding to the root 'ए' in the singular and 'एँ' in the plural; but 'ऊँ' is added when मैं is the subject and 'ओ' when तुम is the subject.

	Singular	Plural
1st Person	मैं आऊँ ? (आ+ऊँ)	हम आएँ (आ+एँ) ?
	1. May I come ?	1. May we come ?
	2. Shall I come ?	2. Shall we come ?
2nd Person	तुम आए , आओ (आ+ए) (आ+ओ).	आप आएँ (आ+एँ).
	1. Please come.	1. Please come.
	2. You may come.	2. You may come.
3rd Person	वह आए (आ+ए)।	वे आएँ (आ+एँ)।
	1. He may come.	1. They may come.
	2. He should come.	2. They should come.
	मैं करूँ (कर+ऊँ)	हम करें (कर+एँ)।
	तू करे (कर+ए)	तुम करो (कर+ओ)।
		आप करें (कर+एँ)।
	वह करे (कर+ए)	वे करें (कर+एँ)।

Vocabulary : Roots

ā	आ	to come	टु कम्
jā	जा	to go	टु गो
kar	कर	to do	टु डू
khel	खेल	o play	टु प्ले
kah	कह	.o say	टु से

bol	बोल	to speak	टु स्पीक्
pī	पी	to drink, to smoke	टु ड्रिंक, टु स्मोक्
khā	खा	to eat	टु ईट्
pa h́	पढ़	to read	टु रीड्
likh́	लिख	to write	टु राइट्
de	दे	to give	टु गिव्
le	ले	go take	टु टेक्
ho	हो	to become,	टु बिकम्,
		to happen	टु हॅप्पन्
dau h́	दौड़	to run	टु रन्

Ishvar kare tuḿ sukhī ho-o !	May God make you happy !
ईश्वर करे तुम सुखी होओ !	मे गॉड् मेक् यू हॅप्पि !
Tumahāre sab́ dukh́ dūr hon̐ !	May all your sorrows be removed !
तुम्हारे सब दुख दूर हों !	मे आल् योर् सॉरोज़् बी रिमूवड् !
Tuḿ Yashasvī ho-o !	May you become illustrious!
तुम यशस्वी होओ !	मे यू बिकम् इलुस्ट्रिअस् !
Chele kī tarakkī hove !	May the disciple prosper !
चेले की तरक्की होवे !	मे दॅ डिसाइपल् प्रॉस्पर् !

Mohań kī unnati na ruke !

मोहन की उन्नति न रुके !

May Mohan's progress be not hindered !

मे मोहनर्स् प्रॉग्रेस बी नॉट् हिंडर्ड् !

Ab́ Rāḿ bāhar ja-e ?

अब राम बाहर जाए ?

May Rāma go out now ?

मे राम गो ऑउट नॉउ ?

Main̐ sabhā men̐ bolūn̐ ?

मैं सभा मैं बोलूँ ?

May I speak at the meeting ?

मे आय् स्पीक् अॅट् द मीटिंग् ?

Ham ise kaise karen̐ ?

हम इसे कैसे करें ?

How shall we do thiś ?

हॉउ शल् वी डू दिस् ?

Ham tumhen̐ akele kaise choh́ den̐ ?

हम तुम्हें अकेले कैसे छोड़ दें ?

How can we leave you alone ?

हॉउ कॅन् वी लीव् यू अलोन् ?

Main̐ kyā sandeśh likh́ bhejūn̐ ?

मैं क्या संदेश लिख भेजूँ ?

What message shall I write and send ?

व्हाट् मेसेज् शल् आय् राइट् अॅण्ड् सेंड् ?

Har ko-ī yaĥ kitāb avaśy pa he.	Everyone should read this book.
हर कोई यह किताब अवश्य पढ़े।	एवरिवन् शुड् रीड् दिस् बुक्।
Āj naukar ghar na jā-e.	Let not the servant go home today.
आज नौकर घर न जाए।	लेट् नॉट् द सर्वेंट् गो होम् टू-डे।
Natkhat laḍkā bench par khaḍā rahe.	Let the naughty boy stand on the bench.
नटखट लड़का बेंच पर खड़ा रहे।	लेट् द नाटि बॉय् स्टैण्ड् ऑन् द बेंच्।
Har ek ādmī apnā-apnā kām kare.	Let each man do his work.
हर एक आदमी अपना-अपना काम करे।	लेट् ईच् मॅन् डू हिज़् वर्क।
Kisī ḍakṭar ko bulāyā jā-e.	Let some doctor be summoned.
किसी डॉक्टर को बुलाया जाए।	लेट् सम् डॉक्टर् बी समन्ड्।

Hamāre mahārājā dīrghjīvī hon̐.	Long live our Mahārājā
हमारे महाराजा दीर्घजीवी हों।	लॉङ्ग् लिव् अवर् महाराजा।
Kaun jāne !	Who knows !
कौन जाने !	व्हू नोज़् !
Maiṇ̐ kyā jānūn̐ ?	What do I know ?
मैं क्या जानूँ ?	व्हाट् डू आय् नो ?
Aisā ho to.	If it be so
ऐसा हो तो	इफ् इट् बी सो
vah vahān̐ ho to.	If he be there
वह वहाँ हो तो	इफ् ही बी देअ-
Khudā jāne !	God (alone) knows !
खुदा जाने !	गॉड् (अलोन्) नोज़्।
Kahūn̐ to kyā kahūn̐ ?	If I am to speak, what shall I speak ?
कहूँ तो क्या कहूँ ?	इफ् आय् ॲम् टु स्पीक्, व्हाट् शल् आय् स्पीक् ?

Jāūn̐ to kahān̐ jāūn̐ ?	If I am to go, where shall I go ?
जाऊँ तो कहाँ जाऊँ ?	इफ् आय् ॲम् टु गो, व्हेअ-शल् आय् गो ?
Karūn̐ to kyā karūn̐ ?	If I am to do, what shall I do ?
करूँ तो क्या करूँ ?	इफ् आय् ॲम् टु डू, व्हाट् शल् आय् डू ?
Ho na ho.	Be it so or not.
हो न हो।	बी इट् सो ऑ नॉट्।
Paṇḍit ho yā mūrkh	Be he a scholar or a fool.
पंडित हो या मूर्ख।	बी ही अ स्कॉलर् ऑ अ फूल्।
Dost ho yā dushman	Be he a friend or an enemy.
दोस्त हो या दुश्मन	बी ही अ फ्रैंड् ऑ एन एनिमि.
Jo karo.	Whatever you do.
जो करो।	व्हाट्एव्हर् यू डू।
Jo kaho.	Whatever you say.
जो कहो।	व्हाट्एव्हर् यू से।

Tum jo chāho. तुम जो चाहो।	Whatever you wish (like). व्हाट्एव्हर् यू विश् (लाइक्).
Agar vahān̐ umada aur mīṭhe ām milen̐ अगर वहाँ उमदा और मीठे आम मिलें.	If good and sweet mangoes are available there. इफ् गुड् ॲण्ड् स्वीट् मॅङ्गोज़् आ´ अव्हेलेबल् देअ´-
Main̐ jāūn̐ aur āp ke liye kuchh seb aur an̐gūr lāūn̐? मैं जाऊँ और आपके लिए कुछ सेब और अँगूर लाऊँ ?	Shall I go and bring some apples and grapes for you ? शल् आय् गो ॲण्ड् ब्रिंग् सम ॲप्पल्स् ॲण्ड् ग्रेप्स् फॉर् यू ?
Shāyad main̐ kal Kalkattā jā-un̐. शायद मैं कल कलकत्ता जाऊँ.	I may perhaps go to Calcutta tomorrow. आय् मे पर्हॅप्स् गो टु कॅलकटा टुमॉरो।
Agar ve vahān̐ na hon̐. अगर वे वहाँ न हों।	If he is not there. इफ् ही इज़् नॉट् देअ´-

Agar aisā ho.
अगर ऐसा हो।

If it is so.
इफ् इट् इज़् सो.

Agar vaĥ aisā kahe to
tum vahīn̐ raho.
अगर वह ऐसा कहे तो
तुम वहीं रहो।

If he says so, then you
stay there.
इफ् ही सेज़ सो, देन् यू
स्टे देअ.

Agar tum vahān̐
jā-o to Bharat se zarūr
milo.
अगर तुम वहाँ
जाओ तो भरत से ज़रूर
मिलो।

If you go there,meet
Bharata positively.
इफ् यू गो देअ, मीट्
भरत पॉज़िटिव्लि।

Tum suno yā na suno,
main̐ yah kahta hūn̐.
तुम सुनो या न सुनो,
मैं यह कहता हूँ।

Whether you hear or not, I
say this.
व्हेदर् यू हिअ ऑ नॉट्, आय्
से दिस्।

Vah āj ghar na jāve.

वह आज घर न जावे।

Let him not go home
today.
लेट् हिम् नॉट् गो होम्
टु-डे।

Habitual Tenses (Simple Tenses) : सामान्यकाल

Habitual tenses are formed by conjugating the present paritciple with the appropriate auxiliary verb.

1. Present Habitual Tense : सामान्य वर्तमान काल
2. Past Habitual Tense : सामान्य भूतकाल
3. Future Habitual Tense : सामान्य भविष्य काल

The present Habitual Tense is rendered into English by Present-Indefinite Tense.

The past Habitual Tense is rendered into English by Past-Indefinite Tense or a special mode—I used to come.

The Future Indefinite Tense is not commonly used. Its purpose is served by the Future Continuous Tense.

Present Habitual Tense : सामान्य वर्तमानकाल

The Present Habitual Tenses are formed by conjugating the Present Participle with Present-Indicative Auxiliarly Verbs — हूँ, है, हैं and हो.

[Present-Participle + Auxiliary Verb Present Indicative].

main̐ ātā hūn̐	मैं आता हूँ	I come
tū ātā hai	तू आता है	Thou come

vah ātā hai	वह आता है	He comes
ham āte hain	हम आते हैं	We come
tum āte ho	तुम आते हो	You come
āp āte hain	आप आते हैं	You come
ve āte hain	वे आते हैं	They come
main ātī hūn	मैं आती हूँ	I come
tū ātī hai	तू आती है	Thou come
vah ātī hai	वह आती है	She comes
ham ātī hain	हम आती हैं	We come
tum ātī ho	तुम आती हो	You come
āp ātī hain	आप आती हैं	You come
ve ātī hain	वे आती हैं	They come

The Past Habitual Tense : सामान्य भूतकाल

[Present Participle + Auxiliary verb –Past Indicative]

main ātā thā	मैं आता था	I used to come
tū ātā thā	तू आता था	Thou used to come
vah ātā thā	वह आता था	He used to come
ham āte the	हम आते थे	We used to come
tum āte the	तुम आते थे	You used to come
āp āte the	आप आते थे	You used to come
ve āte the	वे आते थे	They used to come
main ātī thī	मैं आती थी	I used to come
tū ātī thī	तू आती थी	Thou used to come

vah́ ātī thī	वह आती थी	She used to come
ham ātī thīn̈	हम आती थीं	We used to come
tum ātī thīn̈	तुम आती थीं	You used to come
āṕ ātī thīn̈	आप आती थीं	You used to come
ve ātī thīn̈	वे आती थीं	They used to come

The Future Habitual Tense : सामान्य भविष्यत्काल.

[Present Participle + Auxiliary Verb—Future Indicative]

main̈ ātā hūn̈gā	मैं आता हूँगा
tū ātā hogā	तू आता होगा
vah́ ātā hogā	वह आता होगा
ham āte ho ge	हम आते होंगे
tum āte hoge	तुम आते होगे
āṕ āte ho ge	आप आते होंगे
ve āte ho ge	वे आते होंगे
main̈ ātī hū gī	मैं आती हूँगी
tū ātī hogī	तू आती होगी
vah́ ātī hogī	वह आती होगी
ham ātī ho gī	हम आती होंगी
tum ātī hogī	तुम आती होगी
āṕ ātī ho gī	आप आती होंगी
ve ātī ho gī	वे आती होंगी

The Continuous Tenses : अपूर्णकाल

In continuous Tenses, the root is followed by रहा (rahā) the past participle of रह and a required auxiliary verb.

The continuous tenses are formed by adding रहा (rahā) the past participle of रह, which changes into रहे (rahe) in plural and रही (rahī) in feminine singular and plural, to the root of a verb, followed by the (required) auxiliary verb हो indicating the tense according to the gender, number and person of the subject.

[Root + रहा (rahā) + Auxiliary verb हो—Tense Indicative]

Present Continuous Tense : अपूर्ण वर्तमानकाल

[Root + रहा + Auxiliary verb हो—Present Indicative]

maiṅ ā rahā hūṅ	मैं (m.) आ रहा हूँ	I am coming
tū ā rahā hai	तू (m.) आ रहा है	Thou art coming
vah ā rahā hai	वह (m.) आ रहा है	He is coming
ham ārahe haiṅ	हम (m.) आ रहे हैं	We are coming
tum ārahe ho	तुम (m.) आ रहे हो	You are coming
āp ā rahe haiṅ	आप (m.) आ रहे हैं	You are coming
ve ā rahe haiṅ	वे (m.) आ रहे हैं	They are coming
maiṅ ā rahī hūṅ	मैं (f.) आ रही हूँ	I am coming

tū ā rahī hai	तू (f.) आ रही है	Thou art coming
vah ā rahī hai	वह (f.) आ रही है	She is coming
ham ārahī hain̐	हम (f.) आ रही हैं	We are coming
tum ārahī ho	तुम (f.) आ रही हो	You are coming
āp ā rahī hain̐	आप (f.) आ रही हैं	You are coming
ve ā rahī hain̐	वे (f.) आ रही हैं	They are coming

Past Continuous Tense : अपूर्ण भूतकाल

[Root + रहा (rahā) + Auxiliary verb हो — Past Indicative]

main̐ ā rahā thā	मैं (m.) आ रहा था	I was coming
tū ā rahā thā	तू (m.) आ रहा था	Thou wert coming
vah ā rahā thā	वह (m.) आ रहा था	He was coming
ham ārahe the	हम (m.) आ रहे थे	We were coming
tum ārahe the	तुम (m.) आ रहे थे	You were coming
āp ā rahe the	आप (m.) आ रहे थे	You were coming
ve ā rahe the	वे (m.) आ रहे थे	They were coming
main̐ ā rahī thī	मैं (f.) आ रही थी	I was coming
tū ā rahī thī	तू (f.) आ रही थी	Thou wert coming
vah ā rahī thī	वह (f.) आ रही थी	She was coming.
ham ārahī thin̐	हम (f.) आ रही थीं	We were coming
tum ārahī thin̐	तुम (f.) आ रही थीं	You were coming
āp ā rahī thin̐	आप (f.) आ रही थीं	You were coming
ve ā rahī thin̐	वे (f.) आ रही थीं	They were coming

Future Continuous Tense : अपूर्ण भविष्यत्काल

[Root + रहा (rahā) + Auxiliary verb हो — Future Indicative]

maiṅ ā rahā hūṅgā	मैं (m.) आ रहा हूँगा	I shall be coming
tū ā rahā hogā	तू (m.) आ रहा होगा	Thou wilt be coming
vah ā rahā hogā	वह (m.) आ रहा होगा	He will be coming
ham ā rahe ho ge	हम (m.) आ रहे होंगे	We shall be coming
tum ā rahe ho ge	तुम (m.) आ रहे होंगे	You will be coming
āp ā rahe ho ge	आप (m.) आ रहे होंगे	You will be coming
ve ā rahe ho ge	वे (m.) आ रहे होंगे	They will be coming
maiṅ ā rahī	मैं (f.) आ रही	I shall be

hūngī	हूँगी	coming
tū ā rahī hogī	तू (f.) आ रही होगी	Thou will be coming
vaḥ ā rahī hogī	वह (f.) आ रही होगी	She will be coming
ham ā rahī ho gī	हम (f.) आ रही होंगी	We shall be coming
tum ā rahī ho gī	तुम (f.) आ रही होंगी	You will be coming
āp ā rahī ho gī	आप (f.) आ रही होंगी	You will be coming
ve ā rahī ho gī	वे (f.) आ रही होंगी	They will be coming

The Perfect Tenses : पूर्णकाल

The Perfect Tenses are formed by adding the required tense indicative form of auxiliary verb हो according to the gender and number of the subject to the Past Participle of the root of a verb; *e.g.*,

The Present Perfect Tense : पूर्ण वर्तमानकाल

[Past Participle + Auxiliary Verb हो — Present Indicative]

1. Maiṅ मैं	āyā/āyī hūṅ आया/आयी हूँ	आय् हॅव् कम् I have come
2. Tū/Vah तू /वह	āyā/āyī hai आया/आयी है	दाऊ/ही, शी...../हॅज् कम् Thou/He, She..../has come
3. Tum तुम	āye/āyī ho आये/आयी हो	यू हॅव् कम् You have come
4. Ham/ āp /ve हम/आप/वे	āye/āyī hain आये/आयी हैं	वी/यू/दे हॅव् कम् We/You/They have come

The Past Perfect Tense : पूर्ण भूतकाल

[Past Participle + Auxiliary Verb हो — Past Indicative]

Maiṅ/Tū/Vah मैं/तू/वह	आया/आयी था/थी āyā/āyī thā/thī	आय्/दाऊ/ही, शी I/Thou/He/She	had come हॅड् कम्
Ham/Tum/ Āp/Ve हम/तुम/आप/वे	आये/आयी थे/ थीं āye/āyī the/thīṅ	वी/यू/ यू/दे We/You/ You/They	They had come दे हॅड् कम्

The Future Perfect Tense : पूर्ण भविष्यत्काल

[Past Participle + Auxiliary Verb हो — Future Indicative]

Maiṅ मैं	āyā/āyī hūṅgā/hūṅgī आया/आयी हूँगा/हूँगी	आय् शल् हॅव् कम् I shall have come
Tū/Vaḥ तू/वह	āyā/āyī hogā/hogī आया/आयी होगा/होगी	दाऊ/ही, शी विल्ट्/विल् हॅव् कम् Thou/He, She wilt/will have come
Tuṁ तुम	āye/āyī ho ge/hoṅgī आये/आयी होगे/होगी	यू विल् हॅव् कम् You will have come
Haṁ / Āp/Ve हम/ आप/वे	āye/āyī ho ge/ho gī आये/आयी होंगे/होंगी	वी/यू/दे शल्/विल् हॅव् कम् We/You/They Shall/will have come

Auxiliary Verbs : सहायक क्रियाएँ

सक, चुक, लग, दे, पा, यह, हो, कर, रह and जा are used as auxiliary verb to supplement the principal verb. In such cases it is the auxiliary verb that is subject to inflection, while the principal verb remains unchanged.

(1) सक (saka) is added to root of a verb to mean can or may, *i.e.* to indicate ability or permission. *e.g.*,

Vaḥ kyā kar saktā hai ?	वह क्या कर सकता है ?	What can he do ?

maiṅ yah kām kar saktā hūṅ	मैं यह काम कर सकता हूँ।	I can do this work.
tum Hindi bol sakte ho?	तुम हिन्दी बोल सकते हो ?	Can you speak Hindi ?
tum jā sakte ho.	तुम जा सकते हो।	You may go.
maiṅ vahāṅ nahīṅ jā sakā.	मैं वहाँ नहीं जा सका।	I could not go there.

(2) चुक is added with a root to indicate the completion of an action, *e.g.*,

maiṅ likh chukā	मैं लिख चुका।	I have finished writing.
vah pa h chukī	वह पढ़ चुकी।	She finished reading.
tum kah chukī ho	तुम कह चुकी हो।	You had said.
ve bol chuke the	वे बोल चुके थे।	They had fin--ished speaking.

Ab́ ve gā chuke ho ge	अब वे गा चुके होंगे।	They would have finished singing by now.

ने is not used with the subject, when सक and चुक are used as auxiliaries in the past tense; *e.g.*,

Vaḣ kām̃ kar sakā.	वह काम कर सका।	He could work.
Sīta khā chukī.	सीता खा चुकी।	Sita finished eating.

Note :-The nagative नहीं is best placed between the component parts of a compound verb, *e.g.*,

Tīn mahīne pahile Bholā Hindi boĺ nahĩn sakt́ā thā.
तीन महीने पहले भोला हिन्दी बोल नहीं सकता था।
Bhola could not speak Hindi three months ago.

(3) लग is used with modified infinitive (ना become ने) to express the sense to begin, *e.g.*,

मुरली गाने लगा।	Muralī began to sing.
बच्ची रोने लगी।	The baby (girl) began to cry.

Note :- ने is not used with the subject in the past tense when लग is an auxiliary verb, *e.g.*, राम खाने लगा (न कि राम ने खाने लगा) Rāma began to eat.

(4) दे is used with the modified infinitive to mean 'let' or allow, *e.g.*,

muze jāne do.	मुझे जाने दो।	Let me go.
usko bolne dījiye.	उसको बोलने दीजिये।	Please let him speak.

Note :- When दे is in the past tense, ने is used with the subject, irrespective of the principal verb.

maine usko rahne diyā.	मैंनें उसको रहने दिया।	I permitted him to stay.
Usne muze jāne diyā.	उसने मुझे जाने दिया।	He allowed me to go.
Main ne Gopal ko ander āne diyā.	मैंने गोपाल को अन्दर आने दिया।	I let Gopāl come inside.

(5) पा is used after the root of a verb or with the modified infinitive to mean 'manage to' (ability to do a thing).

कर पाना या करने पाना = to manage to.

मैं वहाँ पहुँच नहीं पाया या पहुंचने नहीं पाया।	I could not manage to reach there.
तुम सुन नहीं पाओगे या सुनने नहीं पाओगे।	You will not be able to hear.

(6) 'चाह' is used with infinitive to indicate desire; *e.g.*,

मैं गाना चाहता हूँ।	I want to sing.

'चाह' is used with past tense to indicate an action about to take place, *e.g.*,

घड़ी में चार बजा चाहते हैं	Th clock is about to strike four.
यह टूटा-फूटा मकान गिरा चाहता है।	This dilapidated house is about to fall

(7) When 'पड़' is used with the infinitive to express force or compulsion, the subject remains in the dative case, and the verb agrees with the object in gender and number.

उसे दवा खानी पड़ी।	He had to take medicine.
मुझे बंबई जाना पड़ता है।	I have to go to Bombay.

मुझे यात्रा मैं बासी रोटियाँ खानी पड़ीं। I had to eat stale bread during the journey.

(8) When हो is used with the infinitive to indicate the necessity of performing an action, the subject takes the dative case and the verb agrees with the object (if any) in gender and number.

मुझे जाना है। I have to go.
उसको दिल्ली जाना था। He had to go to Delhi.
तुमको रोटी खानी होगी। You will have to eat bread.

(9) 'कर' is added as auxiliary to a verb in the past tense to indicate the habitual tense.

पढ़ा करो। Be (in the habit of) reading.
देखा करो। Be (in the habit of) seeing.
वह आया करता है। He habitually comes.
यह काम किया करो। Do this work regularly.

Note :- ने is not used in the habitual past tense.

(10) रह is used with the present or past participle of a verb to express continuity of an action.

तुम बड़बड़ाते रहते हो। You go on murmuring.
सीता हँसती रहती है। Sītā goes on laughing.

Adverbs (ॲड् वर्ब) : क्रिया विशेषण

kab́	कब	When	व्हेन्
kahān̐	कहाँ	Where	व्हेअ́
kyon̐	क्यों	Why	व्हाय्
kaise	कैसे	How	हाउ
kahān̐ se	कहाँ से	Whence	व्हेंस्

Tuḿ kab́ uṭh́te ho ?
तुम कब उठते हो ?

When do you get up?
व्हेन् डू यू गेट् अप् ?

Main̐ pān̐cḣ baje uṭh́tā hūn̐.
मैं पाँच बजे उठता हूँ।

I get up at five.
आय् गेट् अप् ॲट् फाइव।

Tuḿ kyon̐ (kiśliye) kheĺte ho ?
तुम क्यों (किसलिये) खेलते हो ?

Why do you play ?
व्हाय् डू यू प्ले ?

Kāraṇ́, muze kheĺnā pasa d hai.
कारण, मुझे खेलना पसंद है।

Because I like to play.
बिकाज़ आय् लाइक् टु प्ले।

Tum̒ kahān̐ rah̒te ho ?	Where do you stay ?
तुम कहाँ रहते हो ?	व्हेअ॑र् डू यू स्टे ?
Main̐ nukkaḍ par rah̒tā hūn̐.	I stay at the corner.
मैं नुक्कड़ पर रहता हूँ।	आय् स्टे अट् द॑ कॉरनर्।
Tum̒ kaise paḍhte ho ?	How do you read ?
तुम कैसे पढ़ते हो ?	हाउ डू यू रीड् ?
Main̐ dhīre-dhīre paḍh̒ta hūn̐.	I read slowly.
मैं धीरे-धीरे पढ़ता हूँ।	आय् रीड् स्लोलि।
Āp̒ kahān̐ se āte hain̐ ?	Whence do you come ?
आप कहाँ से आते हैं ?	व्हेंस्॑ डू यू कम्?
Main̐ kal̒kattā se ā rahā hūn̐.	I come from Calcutta.
मैं कलकत्ता से आ रहा हूँ।	आय् कम्॑ फ्रॉम् कॅलकटा।
Bas̒ men̐ kit̒ne ād̒mī hain̐ ?	How many men are in the bus ?

बस मैं कितने आदमी हैं ?	हाउ मेनि मेन आॅ इन् दॅ बस् ?
Iś samay ́bać men̐ chalīś ādmī hain̐. इस समय बस में चालीस आदमी हैं।	There are forty men in th bus at present. देअॅ आॅ फोर्टी मेन् इन् दॅ बस अॅट् प्रेज़ेंट.
Tumhen̐ derī kyon̐ huī ? तुम्हें देरी क्यों हुई ?	Why are you late ? व्हाय् आॅ यू लेट् ?
Āṕ <u>kab́</u> ăphiś jāte hain̐ ? आप <u>कब</u> ऑफिस जाते हैं ?	When do you go to office ? व्हेन् डू यू गो टु ऑफिस् ?
Main̐ daś baje ăphiś jātā hūn̐. मैं दस बजे ऑफिस जाता हूँ।	I go to office at ten o'clock. आय् गो टु ऑफिस् अॅट् टेन् ओक्लॉक्.
Āj āṕ kaise hain̐ ? आज आप कैसे हैं ?	How are you today ? हाउ आॅ यू टुडे ?
Main̐ ach-chhā hūn̐. मैं <u>अच्छा</u> हूँ।	I am well. आय् अॅम् वेल्।

Kyā tuḿ hameshā nau baje ghar jāte ho ? क्या तुम हमेशा नौ बजे घर जाते हो ?	Do you always go home at 9 o'clock ? डू यू आलवेज़् गो होम् ॲट् नाइनों क्लॉक ?
Nahīn̐, āj́ vahān̐ kuch́ kāḿ hai. नहीं, आज वहाँ कुछ काम है।	No, today there is some work there. नो, टुडे देअ॔ इज़् सम् वर्क् देअ॔।
Āṕ yahān̐ kab́ se rah́te hain̐ ? आप यहाँ कब से रहते हैं ?	Since when are you living here ? सिंस् व्हेन् आ॔ यू लिविंग् हिअ॔ ?
Main̐ sāt́ diń se yahān̐ rah́tā hūn̐. मैं सात दिन से यहाँ रहता हूँ।	I am living here for the last seven days. आय् ॲम् लिविंग् हिअ॔ फॉ॔ द॔ लास्ट् सेवन् डेज़्.
Vaḣ kiṫnā khātā hai ? वह कितना खाता है ?	How much does he eat ? हाउ मच् डज़् ही ईट् ?
Vaḣ bahuṫ khātā hai. वह बहुत खाता है।	He eats much. ही ईट्स् मच।

Āp pensil se kyon̐ likhte hain̐ ?	Why do you write with a pencil ?
आप पेंसिल से क्यों लिखते हैं ?	व्हाय् डू यू राइट् विद् अ पेंसिल् ?
Āj tum kahān̐ jāte ho ?	Where do you go today ?
आज तुम कहाँ जाते हो ?	व्हेअर् डू यू गो टुडे।
Main̐ āj Bambai jātā hūn̐.	I go to Bombay today.
मैं आज बंबई जाता हूँ।	आय् गो टु बॉम्बे टुडे।
Vah roj yahān̐ kyon̐ ātā hai ?	Why does he come here every day ?
वह रोज यहाँ क्यों आता है?	व्हाय् डज़् ही कम् हिअ एव्रि डे ?
Vah roj nahīn̐ ātā, kabhī-kabhī ātā hai.	He does not come every day, he comes now and then.
वह रोज नहीं आता, कभी-कभी आता है।	ही डज़ नॉट् कम् एव्रि डे, ही कॅमस नॉउ एण्ड देन्.

Post-position : संबंधबोधक

A (Saṁbandh́ bodhaḱ) संबंधबोधक is a word placed after a noun or pronoun to show in what relation (संबंध) the person or thing denoted by it stands in regard to something else and hence it may be called 'Post position', *e.g.*, घर के पास (near the house).

These post-positions are generally preceded by के (ke), की (ki) or से (se), with rare exceptions.

The following are the more important Post-positions :—

1. (के) बाद (bād)— after.

Nau baje ke bād ā-o.	Come after nine o'clock.
नौ बजे के बाद आओ।	कर्म् ऑफ्टर् नाइनों क्लॉक्।

2 (के) पहले (pahle) — before.

Chār baje ke pahle ā-o.	Come before four o'clock.
चार बजे के पहले आओ।	कम् बिफोर् फोरों क्लॉक्।

3. (के) साथ (sāth) — along with.

Bāṕ ke sāth́ tahalne jā-o.	Go for a walk along with father.
बाप के साथ टहलने जाओ।	गो फॉ अ वाक् अलॉङ्ग् विद् फादर्।

4. (के) बिना (binā) — without.

Śakkar ke binā chāý ach-chhī nahīn̐ lagtī.	Tea does not taste well without sugar.
शक्कर के बिना चाय अच्छी नहीं लगती।	टी डज़् नॉट् टेस्ट् वेल् विदॉउट् शुगर्.

5. (के) पास (pāś) — near.

Ghar ke pāś eḱ bāg hai.	There is a garden near the house.
घर के पास एक बाग है।	देअर् इज़् अ गार्डन् निअर् द हॉउस्।

6. (के) विरुद्ध (virud-dh́) — against.

Yah́ niyam ke virud-dh hai.	This is agaist the law.
यह नियम के विरुद्ध है।	दिस् इज़् अगेंस्ट् द लॉ।

7. (के) सामने (sāmne) — in front of.

Mere ghar ke sāmne eḱ nīm kā peḍ hai.	There is a margosa tree in front of my house.
मेरे घर के सामने एक नीम का पेड़ है।	देअर् इज़् अ मार्गोसा ट्री इन् फ्रंट ऑफ् माय् हाउस्.

8. आगे (āge) — further off.

Mere ghar ke āge ek bạḍā bāzār hai.	There is a big bazar further off my house.
मेरे घर के आगे एक बड़ा बाज़ार है।	देअर् इज़् अ बिग् बाज़ार् फर्दर् ऑफ माय् हाउस्।

Conjunction : समुच्चयबोधक

aur	और	And	ॲण्ड्
parantu, magar	परन्तु, मगर	But	बट्
yadi, agar	यदि, अगर	If	इफ्
kyonँki	क्योंकि	Because	बिकाज़
nahīnँ to, anyathā	नहीं तो, अन्यथा	Lest	लेस्ट्
ki, kyonँki	कि, क्योंकि	That	दट्
se, apekṣā se adhik	से, अपेक्षा से अधिक	Than	दॅन्
se, jab se, bād menँ,	से, जब से, बाद में,	Since	सिंस्
tak, jab tak	तक, जब तक	Till	टिल्
jab tak	जब तक	Before	बिफॉर्
tak, jab tak	तक, जब तक	Until	अन्टिल्
bād menँ	बाद में	After	ऑफ्ट्र
yadyapi, māno,	यद्यपि, मानो,	Although	ऑल्दो
hālānँki,	हालाँकि,		
yā, athvā	या, अथवा	Or	ऑ-

Āpke āne tak main̐ yahān̐
   thahrūn̐gā.
आपके आने तक मैं यहाँ
   ठहरूँगा ।

I shall stay here till you
   return.
आय् शल् स्टे हिअॅ टिल् यू
   रिटर्न ।

Dūdh aur rotī
   svāsthyákar anna hai.
दूध और रोटी
   स्वास्थ्यकर अन्न है ।

Milk and bread is
   wholesome food.
मिल्क ऑण्ड् ब्रेड् इज़्
   व्होल् सम् फूड् ।

Ve nahīn̐ āye, kyon̐ki
   āpne unhen̐ bulāyā nahīn̐.
वे नहीं आये, क्योंकि
   आपने उन्हें बुलाया नहीं ।

He did not come because
   you did not call him.
ही डिड् नॉट् कम् बिकाज़्
   यू डिड् नॉट् काल हिम् ।

Yadi āp pakaḍ sakte
   hain̐ to inhen̐ pakaḍiye.
यदि आप पकड़ सकते
   हैं तो इन्हें पकड़िये ।

Catch him, if you can.

कॅच् हिम् इफ् यू कॅन् ।

Unhon̐-ne treń āne tak
   intjār kiyā.
उन्होंने ट्रेन आने तक
   इंतजार किया ।

They waited till the train
   arrived.
दे वेटेड् टिल् द ट्रेन
   अराइव्ड् ।

Kitāb to kitāb hai, hālānँki usँmenँ kuchhँ nahīnँ.	A book is book, although there is nothing in it.
किताब तो किताब है, हालाँकि उसमें कुछ नहीं।	अ बुक् इज़् बुक्, ऑल्दो देअ- इज़् नथिंग् इन् इट्।
Vaĥ kahānī sac-chī hai yā jhūṭhī ?	Is that story true or false ?
वह कहानी सच्ची है या झूठी ?	इज़् दॅट् स्टोरि ट्रू आ फाल्स् ?
Vaĥ garib́ hai, magar hai īmāndār.	He is poor, but he is honest.
वह गरीब है, मगर है ईमानदार।	ही इज़् पुअर्, बट् ही इज़् ऑनेस्ट्।
Ham (isliye) khāte hainँ ki ham jī sakenँ	We eat that we may live.
हम (इसलिये) खाते हैं कि हम जी सकें।	वी ईट् दॅट् वी मे लिव्।

Interjection : विस्मयादिबोधक

In Hindi, there are Interjection : विस्मयादिबोधक (Vismyādi,bodhak) words which express some sudden feeling or emotion. They are not grammatically related to the other words in a sentence.

Chup ! āvāj mat karo. चुप ! आवाज मत करो।	Hush ! Don't make a noise. हश् ! डोंटमेक् अ नाइज़्।
Are ! Vah mar gayī. अरे ! वह मर गयी।	Alas ! She is dead. अलास ! शी इज़् डेड्।
Āh ! Ve chale gaye ? आह ! वे चले गये ?	Ah ! Have they gone ? आह ! हॅव्ह् दे गॉन् ?
Ajī ! Tum vahān kyā kar rahe ho ? अजी ! तुम वहाँ क्या कर रहे हो ?	Hello ! What are you doing there ? हेलो ! व्हाट् आर यू डूइंग् देअर ?
Oh ! Main to bahut ḍar gayā. ओह ! मैं तो बहुत डर गया।	Oh ! I got such a fright. ओह ! आय् गॉट् सच् अ फ्राइट्।
Vāh-vāh ! Hamne khel jīt liyā.	Hurrah ! We have won the game.

वाह–वाह ! हमने खेल जीत लिया।	हुर्रा ! वी हॅव्ह् वन् द गेम् ।
Chhi:-chhi: ! Aisā vyavhār karnā ? छि: छि: ! ऐसा व्यवहार करना ?	Fie ! fie ! Is that the way to behave ? फाइ फाइ ! इज़् दॅट् द वे टु बिहॅव्ह् ?
O ! yahān̐ ā-o ! ओ ! यहाँ आओ !	Hello ! Come here. होला ! कम् हिअ।
Bāp re ! Aisā kyā ? बाप रे ! ऐसा क्या ?	Good heavens ! Is that so ? गुड् हेव्हन्स् ! इज़् दॅट् सो ?
Ajī ! kaho, kaise ho ? अजी ! कहो, कैसे हो ?	Hello ! How are you ? हलो ! हाउ आ यू ?
Śābāś ! Mere dośt ! शाबाश ! मेरे दोस्त !	Well done ! My friend ! वेल् डन् ! माय् फ्रॅण्ड् !
Oh ! Kitnā sundar chitr ! ओह ! कितना सुन्दर चित्र !	Oh ! What a fine picture ! ओह् ! व्हॉट् अ फाइन् पिक्चर् !
Kitnī karuṇā ? कितनी करुणा ?	What a compassion ? व्हॉट् कम्पैशन ?

Kyā khūb ! What excellent !

क्या खूब ! व्हॉट् एक्सेलेंट् !

Passive Voice : कर्मवाच्य

The Passive Voice is rarely used in Hindi. In fact, it is avoided as far as possible and used only when the doer is not mentioned or is not known.

In Passive Voice the object becomes the subject and the verb agrees with the object in gender and number and the subject stands in the Instrumental Case followed by 'से'

e.g. Active Voice : हम दूध में शक्कर डालते हैं।
We add sugar to milk.

Passive Voice : दूध में हमसे शक्कर डाली जाती है।
Sugar is added to milk by us.

The Past Participle as principal verb is subjoined by the tense indicating form of the root 'जा' (ja) duly inflected according to the number and gender of the subject, *e.g.*,

Active Voice : Main̐ phal khātā hūn̐. I eat fruits.
मैं फल खाता हूँ।

Passive Voice : Muzse phal khāye jāte hain̐. The fruits are eaten by me.
मुझसे फल खाये जाते हैं।

Active Voice:	Us'ne (mujhe) pustak' di उसने (मुझे) पुस्तक दी।	He gave me a book.
Passive Voice:	(Mujhe) pustak' di gayī. (मुझे) पुस्तक दी गयी।	A book was given to me. or I was given a book.
Active Voice :	Maiṅ patra likhūṅgā. मैं पत्र लिखूँगा।	I shall write a letter
Passive Voice :	Muzse Patra likhā jā-e-gā. मुझसे पत्र लिखा जाएगा।	The letter will be written by me.

Note: The Passive Voice can be formed from transitive verbs only. But the following intransitive verbs are used in the passive sense.

धुलना	to be washed	छूटना	to be left, to be cured, to be released.
खुलना	to be opened		
खपना	to be sold out.	फूटना	to be broken
बजना	to ring.	टूटना	to be broken

4 TOPICS OF CONVERSATION : बातचीत के प्रकरण

AT A GLANCE

Elementary	: सामान्य
Imperative Sentences	: आज्ञार्थक वाक्य
Questions and answers	: प्रश्न और उत्तर
What"s the Time ?	: कितने बजे हैं ?
A Talk with a Stranger	: एक अपरिचित से बातचीत
At the Barber's	: हज्जाम की दुकान में
At the Laundry Dry cleaner's	: धोबी की दुकान में
At the Tailor's	: दर्जी की दुकान में
At the Shoemaker's	: जूते वाले की दुकान में
At the Doctor's	: डॉक्टर के यहाँ
Asking the way	: रास्ता पूछना
Railway journey	: रेल यात्रा
Reservation of Berth	: आरक्षण
In the Train	: ट्रेन में
Alighting from the train	: ट्रेन से उतरना
By Bus	: बस से
By Taxi	: टैक्सी से

4 TOPICS OF CONVERSATION : बातचीत के प्रकरण

By Steamer-boat	: स्टीमर-बोट से
To open an account in Bank	: बैंक में खाता खोलना
Withdrawal of the money	: बैंक से पैसे निकालना
Deposit of money in the Bank	: बैंक में पैसे जमा करवाना
Crediting the cheque in the Bank	: बैंक में चेक जमा करवाना
Encashment of the Cheque	: चेक का भुगतान
Loan from a Bank	: बैंक से कर्ज
At the Post - office	: डाक - घर में
Telephone Talk	: टेलिफोन पर बातचीत
At the telegraph - Office	: तार-घर में
At the Restaurant	: रेस्टरॉ में
At the Hotel	: होटल में
At the watch-maker's	: घड़ीसाज की दुकान में
At the cloth-shop	: कपड़े की दुकान में
At the green grocer's	: शाक-सब्जी की दुकान में
Seasons	: मौसम ऋतु

AT A GLANCE

Elementary : सामान्य

1. Sāhab́ hain ? — Is the boss in ?
साहब हैं ? — इज़् द बॉस् इन् ?

2. Kaun hai ? — Who is it ?
कौन है ? — व्हू इज़् इट् ?

3. Main̈ Bābū hun̆. — It's Babu.
मैं बाबू हूँ । — इट्ज़् बाबू ।

4. Kyā hai ? — What is it ?
क्या है ? — व्हाट् इज़् इट् ?

5. Kyā hu-ā ? — What happened ?
क्या हुआ ? — व्हाट् हॅप्पन्ड् ?

6. Kuchh́ Nahin̈. — Nothing.
कुछ नहीं । — नथिंग ।

7. Main̈ jā-ūn̈ ? — May I go ?
मैं जाऊँ ? — मे आय् गो ?

8. Vāpaś ānā. — Please come back.
वापस आना । — प्लीज़ कम् बैक् ।

9.	Jaldī ānā. जल्दी आना ।	Come soon. कम् सून् ।
10.	Bahut ach-chhā. बहुत अच्छा ।	As you say, Sir. ॲज़् यू से, सर् ।
11.	Kab āye ? कब आये ?	When did you arrive ? व्हेन् डिड् यू अराइव् ?
12.	Kal. कल।	Yesterday. यस्टर्डे ।
13.	Kaise ho ? कैसे हो ?	How are you ? हाउ आर् यू ?
14	Ach-chhā hūn̐. अच्छा हूँ ।	I am well. आय ॲम् वेल् ।
15.	Jāne dījiye. जाने दीजिये ।	Let it pass. लेट् इट् पास् ।
16.	Main̐ la-ūn ? मैं लाऊँ ?	Shall I bring it ? शल आय् ब्रिंग् इट् ?

17.	Śābās ! शाबाश !	Well done ! Bravo ! वेल् डन ! ब्रेवो !
18.	Vāh́-Vāh́ ! वाह, वाह !	Marvellous ! मार्वेलस् !
19.	Dhany vād́. धन्यवाद ।	Thank you. थैङ्क् यू ।
20.	Aph́soś. अफ़्सोस ।	Sorry. सॉरि ।
21.	Maph́ kījiye. माफ कीजिये ।	Excuse me. एक्स्क्यूज़ मी ।
22.	Kyā khūb́ ! क्या खूब !	How excellent ! हाउ एक्सेलेंट् ।
23.	Namaste. नमस्ते ।	Good-bye. गुड् बाय् ।
24.	Samajhe ? समझे ?	Do you understand ? डू यू अंडरस्टॅण्ड् ?

25. Hān̐ jī !
हाँ, जी !

Yes, I do.
येस्, आय् डू ।

26. Sāl mubārak.
साल मुबारक ।

Happy New Year.
हैप्पि न्यू यीअर ।

27. Kyā phāyadā ?
क्या फायदा ?

What is the use ?
व्हाट् इज़् दॅ यूज़् ?

28. Suniye to.
सुनिये तो ।

Just listen.
जस्ट् लिसन् ।

29. Abhī āyā.
अभी आया ।

(I'm) Coming just now.
(आय्'म्) कमिंग् जस्ट् नाउ ।

30. Dīyā Jalā do.
दीया जला दो ।

Switch on the lamp.
स्विच् ऑन् दॅ लैम्प् ।

31. Dīyā bujhā do.
दीया बुझा दो ।

Switch off the lamp.
स्विच् ऑफ् दॅ लॅम्प् ।

32. Pa khā chalā do.
पंखा चला दो ।

Switch on the fan.
स्विच् ऑन् दॅ फॅन् ।

Imperative Sentences. : आज्ञार्थक वाक्य

Kaṕḍe dho-o.
कपड़े धोओ ।

Wash the Clothes.
वाश् दॅ क्लोद्स् ।

Kaṕḍe badĺo
कपड़े बदलो ।

Change (your) Clothes
चेंज (यॉ-र्) क्लोद्स् ।

Kaṕḍe pah́no.
कपड़े पहनो ।

Put on (your) Clothes.
पुट् ऑन् (यॉ-र्) क्लोद्स् ।

Bāzāŕ jāo.
बाज़ार जाओ ।

Go to the market.
गो टु दॅ मार्केट् ।

Sabjī lāo.
सब्जी लाओ ।

Bring Vegetables.
ब्रिंग वेजिटेबल्स् ।

Khānā pakāo.
खाना पकाओ ।

Cook the food.
कुक् दॅ फूड् ।

Khānā paŕso.
खाना परसो ।

Serve the meal.
सर्व दॅ मील ।

Bāhaŕ jāo.
बाहर जाओ ।

Go out.
गो आउट् ।

Chāý pio. चाय पिओ ।	Have tea. हैव् टी ।
Khiḍkī kholo. खिड़की खोलो ।	Open the window. ओपन् दॅ विंडो।
Dařvājā band karo. दरवाजा बंद करो ।	Shut the door. शट् दॅ डोॅर- ।
Tālā lagāo. ताला लगाओ ।	Lock it. लॉक् इट् ।
Jaldī mať karo. जल्दी मत करो ।	Don't make haste. डोंट् मेक् हेस्ट॑।
Dhīre-dhīre chalo. धीरे-धीरे चलो ।	Walk slowly. वाक् स्लोव्ली ।
Āhistā bolo. आहिस्ता बोलो ।	Speak in low tone. स्पीक् इन् लो टोन।
Joŕ se mať bolo. जोर से मत बोलो ।	Don't speak loudly. डोंट् स्पीक लाउड्ली ।
Dūśrā lāo. दूसरा लाओ ।	Bring another. ब्रिंग अनदर् ।

Bhūlo maṫ.
भूलो मत ।

Don't forget.
डोंट् फॉर्-गेट् ।

Daro maṫ.
डरो मत ।

Don't be afraid.
डोंट् बी अफ्रेड् ।

Shoṙ maṫ karo.
शोर मत करो ।

Don't make a noise.
डोंट् मेक अ नॉयज़ ।

Gandā pānī maṫ pio.
गंदा पानी मत पिओ ।

Don't drink dirty water.
डोंट् ड्रिंक् डर्टी वाटर् ।

Vahān̐ baṙ-baṙ maṫ jāo.
वहाँ बार-बार मत जाओ ।

Don't go there over and over again.
डोंट् गो देअर्- ओवर्- ॲण्ड ओवर्- अगेन् ।

Gaṭhrī uṭháo.
गठरी उठाओ ।

Pick up the bundle.
पिक् अप् द बंडल ।

Gāḍī lāo.
गाड़ी लाओ ।

Bring a Carrige.
ब्रिंग् अ कैरिएज ।

Gāḍī men̐ rakho
गाड़ी में रखो ।

Put it in the Cart.
पुट् इट् इन् द कार्ट् ।

Abhī jāo.	Go atonce.
अभी जाओ ।	गो अट् वन्स् ।
Sīḍhe jāo.	Go straight.
सीधे जाओ ।	गो स्ट्रेट् ।
Dāyen̐ phiro.	Turn to the right.
दायें फिरो ।	टर्न् टु दॅ राइट् ।
Bāyen̐ muḍo	Turn to the left.
बायें मुड़ो ।	टर्न् टु दॅ लेफ्ट् ।
Taiyār karo.	Get (it) ready.
तैयार करो ।	गेट् (इट्) रेडी ।
Pānī ḍālo.	Pour water.
पानी डालो ।	पोर- वाटॅर- ।
Ghaṇti bajāo.	Ring the bell.
घंटी बजाओ ।	रिंग् दॅ बेल् ।
Chup raho.	Shut up.
चुप रहो ।	शट् अप् ।

So Jāo. सो जाओ ।	Go to bed. गो टु बेड् ।
Vilamb mat karo. विलंब मत करो ।	Don't delay. डोंट् डिले ।
Jhāḍū lagāo. झाड़ू लगाओ ।	Sweep the room. स्वीप् द रूम् ।
Taḍke uṭho. तड़के उठो ।	Get up early. गेट् अप् अर्ली ।
Mehnat karo. मेहनत करो ।	Work hard. वर्क् हार्ड ।

Questions and Answers : प्रश्न और उत्तर

Q.	ĀP Kaise hain ? आप कैसे हैं ?	How are you. ? हाउ आर्- यू ?
A.	Bilkul ṭhīk! Dhanyavad. बिल्कुल ठीक । धन्यवाद ।	I am all right. Thanks. आय् ॲम् ऑल् राइट् । थेङ्क्स् ।
Q.	Āpkī umra kyā hai ? आपकी उम्र क्या है ?	How old are you ? हाउ ओल्ड् आर्- यू ?

A.	Merī umar 25 saĺ hai. मेरी उम्र 25 साल है ।	I am twenty-five years old. आय् ॲम् टूवेन्टी–फाइव यीअर्स ओल्ड्।
Q.	Āphiś kaise jāte hain̐ ? ऑफिस कैसे जाते हैं ?	How do you go to office ? हाउ डू यू गो टु ऑफिस ?
A.	Main̐ baś se jātā hūn̐. मैं बस से जाता हूँ ।	I go by bus. आय् गो बाय् बस्।
Q.	Aj́ āṕ kaisā mah́sūś kaŕ rahe hain̐ ? आज आप कैसा महसूस कर रहे हैं ?	How are you feeling today ? हाउ आर्- यू फीलिंग् टु–डे ?
A.	Kāphi beh́taŕ. Dhanyavāď. काफी बेहतर । धन्यवाद ।	Much better. Thank you. मच् बेटर्. थेङ्क् यू।
Q.	Āṕkā uś laḍkī se kyā nātā hai ? आपका उस लड़की से क्या नाता है ?	How are you related to that girl ? हाउ आर्- यू रिलेटेड् टु दैट् गर्ल् ?
A.	vah́ merī bahań hai. वह मेरी बहन है ।	She is my sister. शी इज़् माय् सिस्टर् ।

Q.	Tuṁ kisaṅ ho kya ?	Are you a farmer ?
	तुम किसान हो क्या ?	आर्- यू अ फार्मर'- ?
A.	Han / Nahin̐.	Yes, I am./No, I am not.
	हाँ / नहीं।	यस्, ऑय्अॅम् / नो, आय्अॅम् नॉट्।
Q.	Tuṁ ja rahe ho ?	Are you going ?
	तुम जा रहे हो ?	आर्- यू गोइंग् ?
A.	Han̐ /Nahin̐.	Yes, I am. / No, I am not.
	हाँ / नहीं।	यस् आय्अॅम्. / नो, आय्अॅम् नॉट्.
Q.	Tuṁ uśke bhaī ho kyā ?	Are you her brother ?
	तुम उसके भाई हो क्या ?	आर्- यू हर ब्रदर्- ?
A.	Han̐ / Nahin̐.	yes, I am. / No, I am not.
	हाँ / नहीं।	यस्, आय् अॅम्। /नो, आय् अॅम् नॉट्।
Q.	Tuṁ mere sāth ā rahe ho kyā ?	Are you coming with me ?
	तुम मेरे साथ आ रहे हो क्या ?	आर्- यू कमिंग् विद् मी ?

A.	Han̐/Nahin̐. हाँ/नहीं।	Yes, I am. No, I am not. यस्, आय् ॲम/नो, आय् ॲम् नॉट्।
Q.	Ham̐ Chalen̐ (kyā) ? हम चलें (क्या) ?	Are we going ? आर्- वी गोइंग् ?
A.	Itne men̐ nahen̐. इतने में नहीं।	No, not yet. नो, नॉट् येट्।
Q.	Hame yahān̐ rahna hai kyā ? हमें यहाँ रहना है क्या ?	Are we staying here ? आर्- वी स्टेइंग् हिअर्- ?
A.	Han̐, beśak. हाँ, बेशक।	Yes, of course ! यस्, ऑफ् कोर्स।
Q.	Uskī madad karni hai kyā ? उसकी मदद करनी है क्या ?	Are we to help him ? आर्- वी टु हेल्प् हिम् ?
A.	Jarūr. जरूर।	Certainly. सरटेन्ली।

Q.	Ham̐ sāth chal rahe hain̐ kyā ? हम साथ चल रहे हैं क्या ?	Are we going together ? आर्- वी गोइंग टु-गेदर्र- ?
A.	Hān̐. हाँ।	I think so. आय थिंक् सो ।
Q.	Ve ab jā rahe hain̐ kyā ? वे अब जा रहे हैं क्या ?	Are they going now ? आर्- दें गोइंग् नाउ ?
A.	Muze nahīn̐ mālūm̐. मुझे नहीं मालूम ।	I don't know. आइ डोंट् नो ।
Q.	Ve yahān̐ rahne vale hain̐ kyā ? वे यहाँ रहने वाले हैं क्या ?	Are they to stay here ? आर् दे टु स्टे हिअर्- ?
A.	Mumkin hai ve rahen̐. Muze nahīn̐ mālūm̐. मुमकिन है वे रहें। मुझे नहीं मालूम।	They may . I don't know. दे मे । आय् डोंट् नो ।

Q.	Ve teniś achchhā khelte hāin kyā ? वे टेनिस अच्छा खेलते हैं क्या ?	Are they good at tennis ? आर्- दे गुड् अॅट् टेनिस् ?
A.	Meri jānkārī men̐ . मेरी जानकारी मे।	I am told so . आय् अम् टोल्ड् सो ।
Q.	Māin̐ jāūn̐/chalūn̐ (kyā) मैं जाऊँ/चलूँ (क्या) ?	Am I to go ? अम् आय् टु गो ?
A.	An̐ hn̐ ! abhī nāhin̐. अं हं ! अभी नहीं।	No, not yet . नो, नॉट् येट् ।
Q.	Kyā main̐ itnā bev'kūf hūn̐ ? क्या मैं इतना बेवकूफ हूँ ?	Am I so foolish ? ॲम् आय् सो फुलिश् ?
A.	Magar kahā kiśne ? मगर कहा किसने ?	Who said so ? व्हू सेड् सो ?
Q.	Māin̐ tumhāre bharose rahūn̐ kyā ? मैं तुम्हारे भरोसे रहूँ क्या ?	Am I to depend on you ? ॲम् आय् टु डिपेंड ऑन् यू ?

A.	Nahīn̐ raho to behtar. नहीं रहो तो बेहतर।	Better not to. बेटर् नॉट् टु।
Q.	Main̐ terā dost hun̐ (kyā)? मै तेरा दोस्त हूँ (क्या) ?	Am I your friend? ॲम् आय् योर् फ्रैंड ?
A.	Tuze hī mālum. तुझे ही मालूम ।	You know best यू नो बेस्ट्।
Q.	Hāmāre sāth nahīn̐ chale ge? हमारे साथ नहीं चलेंगे ?	Won't you come with us? वोंट् यू कम् विद् अस् ?
A.	Nahīn̐; māphī chāhtā hūn̐. नहीं ; माफी चाहता हूँ ।	No, Sorry. नो ; सॉरी ।

What's the Time? : कितने बजे हैं ?

1. Kitne baje hain?/ Kyā samay hai? कितने बजे हैं ? / क्या समय है ?	What is the time? व्हाट् इज द टाइम ?

2. Chār. / Chār baje hain̐. चार ।/ चार बजे हैं ।	It's 4 O'clock. इट्स् फोरों क्लॉक् ।
3. Thīk pān̐ch ./ Thīk pān̐ch baje hain̐. ठीक पाँच ।/ ठीक पाँच बजे हैं ।	It's exactly 5 O'clock. इट्स् ऑक्झक्ट्लि फाइवो क्लॉक ।
4. Sā hh chhá-h ./ Sā hhe chhah baje hain̐. साढे छः ।/ साढे छः बजे हैं ।	It is half past six. इट् इज़् हाफ् पास्ट सिक्स् ।
5. Savā sāt. / Savā sāt baje hain̐. सवा सात ।/ सवा सात बजे हैं ।	It's a quarter past seven. इट्इज़अ क्वार्टर् पास्ट सेवन् ।
6. Paune āṭh/ Paune āṭh baje hain̐. पौने आठ ।/ पौने आठ बजे हैं ।	It's a quarter to eight. इट्स अ क्वार्टर् टु एट् ।
7. Nau ko daś minat. / Nau ko daś minat kam hain̐. नौ में दस मिनट ।/ नौ में दस मिनट कम है	It's ten minutes to nine. इट्स टेन मिनट्स् टु नाइन् ।

8. Daś bājkar pānch minaṭ. / Daś bajkar pānch minaṭ hu-e hain.	It's five minutes past ten.
दस बजकर पाँच मिनट । / दस बजकर पाँच मिनट हुए हैं ।	इट्स फाइव् मिनट्स् पास्ट् टेन् ।
9. Gāḍī gyārah baje din men chhūṭtī hai.	The train leaves at 11.00 a.m.
गाड़ी ग्यारह बजे दिन में छूटती है ।	द ट्रेन लीव्स अॅट् 11.00 ए. एम.
10. Dūkānen bārah baje din men band hotī hain.	Shops are closed at 12 o'clock at mid-day.
दूकानें बारह बजे दिन में बंद होती हैं ।	शॉप्स आ क्लोज़्ड् अॅट् टूवल्व्हो क्लॉक अॅट मिड्-डे ।
11. Ḍākiyā ek baje ātā hai.	The Post man comes at 1 o'clock at noon.
डाकिया एक बजे आता है ।	द पोस्टमॅन् कम्स् अॅट वनों क्लॉक् अॅट् नून् ।
12. Main ḍeḍh baje khānā khātā hūn.	I take lunch at 1. 30 p.m.
मैं डेढ़ बजे खाना खाता हूँ ।	आय् टेक् लंच् अॅट् वन् थर्टी पी.एम.

13. Main̐ do baje dópahaŕ men̐ zapkī letā hūn̐.
मैं दो बजे दोपहर में झपकी लेता हूँ ।

I nap at 2 o'clock afternoon.
आय् नॅप् अॅट् टू ओं'क्लॉक् आफ्टर् नून ।

14. Main̐dh hā-ī baje kăphī- bāŕ jātā hūn̐.
मैं ढाई बजे कॉफी बार जाता हूँ ।

I go to coffee bar at 2.30 p.m.
आय् गो टु कॉफी-बार अॅट टू थर्टी पी.एम.

15. Bach-che skūĺ se tīń baje dopahaŕ men̐ lautte hain̐.
बच्चे स्कूल से तीन बजे दोपहर में लौटते हैं ।

The children return from the school at 3 o'clock afternoon.
द' चिल्ड्रेन् रिटर्न फ्रॉम् द' स्कूल् अॅट् थ्री ओं' क्लॉक आफ्टर्नून् ।

16. Gāḍiyān̐ diń-rāt chaĺtī hain̐.
गड़ियाँ दिन-रात चलती हैं ।

Trains are running day and night.
ट्रेन्स् आ' रनिंग् डे अॅण्ड् नाइट् ।

17. Vah subah ā̆phiś jātī hai āuŕ śāamí ko lauttī hai.
वह सुबह ऑफिस जाती है और शाम को लौटती है ।

She goes to office in the morning and returns in the evening.
शी गोज़् टु ऑफिस् इन् द' मॉर्निंग् अॅण्ड् रिटर्न्स् इन् द' इव्हनिंग् ।

A Talk with a stranger: एक अपरिचित से बातचीत

Apḱā kyā naḿ hai ? आपका क्या नाम है ?	May I know your name, please ? मे आय् नो योर्र नेम्, प्लीज़् ?
Mainँ Somasundaram hūn. मैं सोमसुन्दरम हूँ ।	My name is Somasundaram. माय् नेम् इज़् सोमर्सुन्दरम् ।
Āpkā kārobāŕ kyā hai ? आपका कारोबार क्या है ?	Could I know what you are ? कुड् आय् नो व्हाट् यू आर्- ?
Mainँ in jniar hūnँ. मैं इंजिनियर हूँ ।	I am an engineer. आय् ॲम् अन् इंजिनियर् ।
Āṕke pitā kyā vyavśāyv́ karte hainँ. आपके पिता क्या व्यवसाय करते हैं	What is your father ? व्हाट् इज़् यो‍र्- फादर्- ?
Ve ḍākṭar hainँ. वे डाक्टर हैं ।	He is a doctor . ही इज़् अ डॉक्टर् ।
Āṕ kahānँ se āye hainँ ? आप कहाँ से आये हैं ?	Where are you coming from ? व्हेयर आर्- यू कमिंग फ्रॉम ?

Yahān̐ kiś kāḿ se āye hain̐ ?	What brings you here ?
यहाँ किस काम से आये हैं ?	व्हाट ब्रिंड्स् यू हिअर्-?
Main̐ ek mitt a kī śādī men̐ śarīk hone āya hūn̐.	I have come to attend a friend's wedding.
मैं एक मित्र की शादी में शरीक होने आया हूँ ।	आय हैव्ह कम् टु अटेंड् अ फ्रॅण्ड्स वेडिंग्।
Aur apnī bahán ke lie yogya vaŕ dekh́ne ke liye.	And to look for a suitable match for my sister.
और अपनी बहन के लिए योग्य वर देखने के लिए।	ॲण्ड् टु लुक् फॉर् अ सुटेबल् मॅच् फॉर माय् सिस्टर् ।
Kahin̐ kuchh́ jamā kyā ?	Any luck ?
कहीं कुछ जमा क्या ?	एनी लक ?
Abhi tak to nahin̐.	Not yet.
अभी तक तो नहीं।	नॉट् येट्।
Achchhā, āṕke mitt a kī śādī kab hai ?	I see, when is your friend's wedding ?
अच्छा, आपके मित्र की शादी कब है ?	आय् सी, व्हेन् इज् यों- फ्रैण्ड्स वेडिंग् ?

Kal.	To-morrow.
कल।	टुमारो।
Āp yahān̐ kitne din thahre ge ?	How long will you be here ?
आप यहाँ कितने दिन ठहरेंगे ?	हाऊ लाँग् विल् यू बी हिअ ?
Lagbhag pandrah din.	About two weeks.
लगभग पन्द्रह दिन।	अबाउट् टू वीक्स्।
To āp parson śām ko mere yahān̐ bhojan ko kyon̐ nahīn̐ āte ?	Then why not come to take a chop with me day after to- morrow evening ?
तो आप परसों शाम को मेरे यहाँ भोजन को क्यों नहीं आते ?	देन व्हाय् नॉट् कम् टु टेक् अ चॉप् विद् मी डे आफ्टर् टु-मारो इव्हनिंग् ?
Hān̐, hān̐, avśya āūn̐gā.	The pleasure's mine.
हाँ, हाँ, अवश्य आऊँगा ।	द प्लेजर इज़ माइन।
Āpkī bahan kyā karatī hai ?	What is your sister ?
आपकी बहन क्या करती है ?	व्हाट् इज़् योर् सिस्टर- ?
Vah angrejī kī profesar hain̐.	She is an English-Lecturer.
वह अंग्रेजी की प्रोफेसर है ।	शी इज़् ॲन् इंग्लिश्-लैक्चरर।

Laḍke ke bāre me āpkī kyā apekṣā hai ?	What're your expectations ?
लड़के के बारे में आपकी क्या अपेक्षा है ?	व्हाटार् यो र् एक्स्पेक्टेशन्स ?
Kaṁ se kaṁ M.A.	Must be post-graduate.
कम से कम एम.ए. हो।	मस्ट् बी पोस्ट्-ग्रॅज्युएट्।
Aur kahīn̈ achchhī naukarī ho.	and well fixed up some where.
और कहीं अच्छी नौकरी हो।	ॲण्ड् वेल् फिक्स्ड् अप् सम व्हेअ –।
Āp parson̈ ā rahe hain̈ na ?	You are coming day-after tomorrow is n't it ?
आप परसों आ रहे हैं न ?	यू आ– कमिंग् डे–आफ्ट– टु–मॉरो इज् नॉट् इट् ?
Main̈ ek achchhā-sā parivār dikhāūngā.	I shall suggest you a good family.
मैं एक अच्छा सा परिवार दिखाऊँगा।	ऑय् शल् सजेस्ट् यू अ गुड् फॅमिली।
Dhanyavād. Avaśya āūngā.	Thank you. I will.
धन्यवाद। अवश्य आऊँगा।	थेङ्क् यू। आय् विल्।

Namaskār	Good -day.
नमस्कार	गुड् - डे.
Namaskāŕ.	Good-day
नमस्कार.	गुड्-डे.

At the Barber's: हज्जाम की दुकान में

1.	Muze dā hhī bańvānī hai.	I would like to have shave.
	मुझे दाढ़ी बनवानी है ।	आय् वुड् लाइर्क टु हैव् शेव् ।
2.	Bilkul sāf dā hhī banāo .	Shave me very close.
	बिलकुल साफ दाढ़ी बनाओ	शेव् मी वेरि क्लोज़् ।
3.	Sābuń jarā achchhā lagāo.	Lather it more.
	साबुन ज़रा अच्छा लगाओ ।	लॅदर् इट् मोर् ।
4.	Tumhārā ustárā kund hai.	Your razor is blunt.
	तुम्हारा उस्तरा कुन्द है ।	योर् रेझ़र् इज़् ब्लंट् ।
5.	Dekho, tumhāre ustáre ne kāt diyā hai.	See, your razor has cut here.
	देखो, तुम्हारे उस्तरे ने काट दिया है ।	सी, युओं रेज़र् हॅज़् कट् हिअ .

6. Vahā̃n thoḍī- sī phiṭkarī lagāo.	Would you please apply a bit alum !
वहाँ थोड़ी सी फिटकरी लगाओ ।	वुड् यू प्लीज् अप्लाय् अ बिट् अलम् ।
7. Ustarā tej karo.	Sharpen the razor.
उस्तरा तेज करो ।	शार्पन् दं रेझर् ।
8. Muze keś kaṭvāne hain̐.	I want a hair-cut, please.
मुझे केश कटवाने हैं ।	आय् वांट् अ हेअर्- कट्, प्लीज़् ।
9. Bahut chhoṭe mat kāṭo.	Don't cut it too short.
बहुत छोटे मत काटो ।	डोंट् कट् इट् टू शॉर्ट् ।
10. kain̐chi se hī kāṭo.	Scissors only, please.
कैंची से ही काटो ।	सीजर्स ऑन्ली, प्लीज् ।
11. Yahā̃n jarā aur chhoṭā karo.	A little shorter, here.
यहाँ ज़रा और छोटा करो ।	अ लिट्ल शार्टर्, हिअर् ।

12. Āṕke bāĺ zaḍ rahe hain̐.
आपके बाल झड़ रहे हैं ।

Your hair are falling.
योर्- हेअर्-र्स आर्- फालिंग् ।

13. Kyā āṕne khyāĺ kiyā hai ?
क्या आपने ख्याल किया है ?

Have you noticed it ?
हैव् यू नोटिस्ड् इट् ?

14. Merī samaź men̐ yaḿ maurusī deń hai.
मेरी समझ में यह मौरूसी देन है ।

I think, it is hereditary one.
आय् थिंक्, इट् इज़् हेरिडिटरी वन् ।

15. Kyā koī ilāź kaŕ rahe hain̐ ?
क्या कोई इलाज़ कर रहे हैं ?

Do you take any treatment ?
डू यू टेक एनी ट्रीट्मेंट ?

16. Main̐ ne bahut́ kuchh́ kiyā magaŕ koī natījā nahīn̐.
मैंने बहुत कुछ किया मगर कोई नतीज़ा नहीं ।

I tried a lot, but with no results.
आय् ट्राइड अ लॉट्, बट् विद् नो रिज़ल्ट्स् ।

17. Jarā, merī mūn̐chh́ san̐vāŕ do.
जरा, मेरी मूँछ सँवार दो ।

Would you please trim my moustache
वुड् यू प्लीज़ ट्रिम् माय् मुस्ताच् ?

18. Bilkul ṭhīk. — That's enough off.
बिलकुल ठीक। — दॅट्'ज़् इनफ् ऑफ् ।

19. Bahut hī sundar. — That's fine.
बहुत ही सुंदर । — दॅट्'ज़् फाइन॑ ।

20. Dhanyavād. — Thank you.
धन्यवाद । — थेङ्क् यू ।

21. Muze kitnā denā hai ? — How much do I owe you ?
मुझे कितना देना है ? — हाउ मच् डू आय् ओ यू ?

22. Aur yah tumhāre lie. — And this is for you.
और यह तुम्हारे लिए। — ॲण्ड् दिस् इज़् फॉ- यू।

At the Laundry/ Dry Cleaner's: धोबी की दुकान में

1. Nazdīk meṅ lānḍrī/ḍrāy klīnars kahāṅ hai ? — Where is the nearest laundry/ dry cleaner's ?
नजदीक में लाँड्री/ड्राय क्लीनर्'स् कहाँ है ? — व्हेअर्- इज़् द॑ निअरेस्ट लांड्री/ ड्राय् क्लीनर्'स् ?

2. Muze in kapḍoṅ ko ḍhulāna/istarī karranā hai. — I Want these clothes washed/ ironed (pressed).
मुझे इन कपड़ों को धुलाना/इस्तरी कराना है — आय् वांट् दीज़् क्लोद्स वाश्ड/ आयर्न्ड (प्रेस्ड)।

3. Kab́ milenġe ?
कब मिलेंगे ?

When these will be ready ?
व्हेन दीज़ विल् बी रेडी ?

4. Muze āj́/kal/ śanivāŕ ke pahle chāhiye.
मुझे आज/कल/शनिवार के पहले चाहिये।

I need them today/ tomorrow/before Saturday.
आय् नीड् देम् टुडे/ टुमॉरो/ बिफोर् सटर्डे।

5. Muze ek hafte men jarūŕ chāhiye.
मुझे एक हफ्ते में जरूर चाहिये।

I must have them within a week.
आय् मस्ट् हैव् देम् विदिन् अ वीक्।

6. Bahut kānjī/nīl mat ḍālo.
बहुत काँजी/नील मत डालो ।

Doun't put too much starch/blue.
डोंट् पुट् टू मच् स्टार्च्/ब्लू।

7. (Mere) kapḍe gino.
(मेरे) कपड़े गिनो ।

Count my clothes.
काउंट् माय् क्लोद्ंस् ।

8. Kyā kuchh kam hai ?
क्या कुछ कम है ?

Is there any thing missing ?
इज़् देअर् एनिथिंग् मिसिंग् ?

9. Hān, ek kapḍā kam hai.
हाँ, एक कपड़ा कम है।

Yes, there's one piece missing.
यस्, देअर्-ज़् वन पीस मिसिंग् ।

10. Ṭhīḱ tarah́ se dekho.
ठीक तरह से देखो।

Check them properly.
चेक् देम् प्रॉपर्ली ।

11. Yah́ merī nahīn̈ hai.
यह मेरी नहीं है ।

This is not mine.
दिस् इज़् नॉट् माइन् ।

12. Ye mere rumāl
nahīn̈ hain̈.
ये मेरे रुमाल
नहीं हैं ।

These are not my
handkerchieves.
दीज़् आर् नॉट् माय्
हैंड्कर्चीवस् ।

13. Yah́ kamīz' tumne faḍ
dī hai.
यह कमीज तुमने फाड़
दी है ।

You have torn this shirt.
यू हैव् टॉर्न् दिस् शर्ट् ।

14. Ise sī saḱte ho ?
इसे सी सकते हो ?

Can you stich this ?
कॅन् यू स्टिच् दिस् ?

15. Dikhāi na de, aisā
durusta kar saḱte ho ?
दिखाई न दे, ऐसा
दुरुस्त कर सकते हो ?

Can this be mended
invisibly ?
कॅन् दिस् बी मेन्डेड
इन्विज़िब्ली ?

16. Yah achchhī tarah ḍhulā nahīn hai.
यह अच्छी तरह धुला नहीं है ।

This is not properly washed.
दिस् इज़् नॉट् प्रॉपर्ली वाश्ड् ।

17. Ise vāpas le jao.
इसे वापस ले जाओ।
aur fir dhokar lāo.
और फिर धोकर लाओ ।

Take this back.
टेक् दिस् बॅक्.
And have it washed again.
ॲण्ड् हैव् इट् वाश्ड् अगेन् ।

18. Yah bahut hī naram hai.
यह बहुत ही नरम है ।
Ṭhīk se istarī karo.
ठीक से इस्तरी करो ।

This is too limp.
दिस् इज़् टू लिम्प् ।
Iron it properly.
आयर्न् इट् प्रॉपर्ली ।

19. Yah dāg chhuḍā sakoge ?
यह दाग छुड़ा सकोगे ?

Can you get this stain out ?
कॅन् यू गेट् दिस् स्टेन् आऊट् ?

20. Ismen surākh hai.
इसमें सुराख़ है ।

There is a hole in this.
देअर्- इज़् अ होर्ल इन् दिस् ।

21. Ise pevan lagā sakoge ?
इसे पेवन लगा सकोगे ?

Can you patch this ?
कॅन् यू पॅच् दिस् ?

22. Tuḿne tāuliyā ko jala diyā hai. — You have burnt this towel.
तुमने तौलिये को जला दिया है । — यू हैव् बर्न्ट् दिस् टॉवेल् ।

23. Kyā mere kaṕḍe taiyāŕ hain̐ ? — Is my laundry ready ?
क्या मेरे कपड़े तैयार हैं ? — इज़् माय् लॉंड्री रेडी ?

24. Gāyab́ kaṕḍe jab́ taḱ tuḿ nahīn̐ lāte, tab́ taḱ tumh́en̐ paise nahīn̐ milen̐ge. — I will not pay you until the missing articles are returned.
ǵायब कपड़े जब तक तुम नहीं लाते, तब तक तुम्हें पैसे नहीं मिलेंगे । — आय् विल् नॉट् पे यू अन्‌टिल् दॅ मिसिंग् आर्टिकल्स् आ- रिटर्न्ड् ।

At the Tailor's : दर्जी की दुकान में

1. Namaste, Sāh́b́ ! — Good morning, Sir.
नमस्ते, साहब ! — गुड् मॉर्निंग्, सर् ।

2. Sāh́b kā kyā hukam hai ?	What can I do for you ?
साहब का क्या हुक्म है !	व्हाट् कॅन् आय् डू फॉ- यू ?
3. Muze ek sūt silānā hai.	I should like to be stiched a suit.
मुझे एक सूट सिलाना है।	आय् शुड् लाइक् टु बी स्टिच्ड अ सूट्।
4. Uske lie nāp len̐.	Measure me for the same.
उसके लिए नाप लें।	मेज़र मी फॉ- द सेम्- ।
5. Thīk hai, Sāheb, Āp idhr ā jāen̐.	With pleasure, Sir. Kindly step this way.
ठीक है, साहब, आप इधर आ जाएँ।	विद् प्लेज़र्, सर्। काइंड्ली स्टेप् दिस् वे।
6. Āp kis dha g ka sūṭ pasaṇd karte hain̐ ?	What style would you prefer ?
आप किस ढंग का सूट पसन्द करते हैं ?	व्हाट् स्टाइल् वुड् यू प्रिफर् ?
7. Muze achchhe ṭerilin kā sūṭ silānā hai !	I want a suit of good terylene.
मुझे अच्छे टेरिलिन का सूट सिलाना है।	आय् वांट् अ सूट् ऑफ् गुड् टेरिलिन्।

8. Āṕke pāś ṭeriliń ke achchhe namūne hain̐ kyā ?	Have you a good samples of terylene with you ?
आपके पास टेरिलिन के अच्छे नमूने हैं क्या ?	हैव् यू अ गुड् सैंपल्स ऑफ टेरिलिन् विद् यू
५. Jarūŕ Sāh́ab́. koī khāś ra g ?	Certainly, Sir, any particular colour ?
ज़रूर साहब, कोई खास रंग ?	सर्टेन्ली, सर्. एनी पर्टिकुलर कलर ?
10. Han̐, Muze gaḿrā (gārḥa) sūn̐ghnī kā ra g chāhiye.	Yes, I want a dark brown.
हाँ, मुझे गहरा (गाढ़ा) सुँधनी का रंग चाहिए।	यस्, आय् वाट् अ डार्क ब्राउन्।
11. Yaḿ bahuṫ hī achchhā kapḋā hai, Sahab́, ṭiḱne men̐ maźbūt́ dikh́ne men̐ achchhā.	Here is a very nice cloth, Sir, wears well and looks neat.
यह बहुत ही अच्छा कपड़ा है, साहब, टिकने में मजबूत, दिखने में अच्छा।	हिअर्- इज़् अ व्हेरि नाइस क्लॉथ्, सर्, वेअर्स् वेल् अ‍ॅण्ड लुक्स् नीट्।

Hān̐, yaĥ achchhā lagta hai, magar jarā bhāri malūm pa tā hai.	Yes, that's quite nice. But it is rather heavy.
हाँ, यह अच्छा लगता है, मगर जरा भारी मालूम पड़ता है.	यस्, दैट् स् क्वाएट् नाइस्. बट् इट् इज़् रादर् हेवी।
Isse—Iskī apekṣā halka nahīn hai kyā ?	Haven't you anything lighter ?
इससे—इसकी अपेक्षा हल्का नहीं है क्या ?	हॅव्हन् ट् यू एनिथिङ्ग् लाइटर् ?
Jī hān̐, yaĥ dekhiye— yaĥ bahut hī behtarīn kapḍā hai.	Yes Sir, here is some really nice stuff.
जी हाँ, यह देखिए— यह बहुत ही बेहतरीन कपड़ा है।	यस् सर्, हिअर्- इज़् सम् रिअली नाइस् स्टफ्।
Yaĥ jarā mahangā jarūr hai, magar kapḍa dekhen̐ to maha gā nahīn̐.	It is a bit more expensive, but it is worth the extra money.
यह जरा महँगा ज़रूर है, मगर कपड़ा देखें तो महँगा नहीं।	इट् इज़् अ बिट् मोर् एक्स्पेन्सिव्, बट् इट् इज़् वर्थ् द एक्स्ट्रा मनि।

Kyā bhāv hai ?
क्या भाव है ?

What's the price ?
व्हाट् स् द प्राइस् ?

.... Rupye mītar.
.... रुपये मीटर।

Rs. .... a meter, Sir.
रु० ....अ मीटर्, सर्।

Sūt ke lie kul
kitnā kapḍā lagegā ?
सूट के लिए कुल
कितना कपड़ा लगेगा ?

How much should I require
for a suit ?
हाउ मच् शुड् आय् रिक्वायरं
फॉर अ सूट् ?

Sā he tīn mītar
kāfī hai.
साढ़े तीन मीटर
काफी है.

Three metres and a half would
be ample.
थ्री मीटर्स ॲण्ड अ हाफ् वुड्
बी ॲम्पल्।

Matlab yah ki kapḍe kī
kīmat Rapuye hogī.
मतलब यह कि कपड़े की
कीमत रुपये होगी।

It means cloth shall cost me
Rs.
इट् मीन्स क्लाथ शैल कॉस्ट मी
रु०

I see. That will be Rs.......
P. altogether.
आय् सी. दैट् विल् बी रु०.........
पै. आलटुगेदर्.

Is kapḍe kī ṣiphāriṣ main̐ purṇ rūp se karū̃ gā.
इस कपड़े की सिफारिश मैं पूर्ण रूप से करूँगा।

This is a cloth I can thoroughly recommend.
दिस् इज़् अ क्लॉथ् आय् कॅन् थॅारोलि रिकमेंड।

Aur sūt kī silāī kitnī hogī ?
और सूट की सिलाई कितनी होगी ?

And what would you charge for the making ?
अॅण्ड व्हाट् वुड् यू चार्ज फॉ- दं मेकिंग् ?

Sirph.....rupye sāhab.
सिर्फ......रुपये, साहब.

Only..... Rs, Sir.
ऑन्ली रुपीज़ सर्।

Achchhā, matalab ye ki kul milākar rupye ho ge, ṭhīk hai !
अच्छा, मतलब ये कि कुल मिलाकर रुपये होंगे, ठीक है।

Ṭhīk hai. ठीक है।	Alright आल्राइट्
Hañ] main ise he launga. हां, मैं इसे ही लूंगा।	I think I will take it. आय् थिंक् आय् विल् टेक् इट्.
Bahut achchhā Sāhb. ab āpkā nāp letā hun̐. Dhanyavād. बहुत अच्छा साहबं अब आपका नाप लेता हूँ। धन्यवाद।	Very good, Sir. I will take your measurements. वेरी गुड्, सर्. आय् विल् टेक् यों- मेज़र मेन्ट्स।
Kapḍe kī silāī ka kamī-jyādā dekhne ke lie āp Somvār ko ā sake ge ? कपड़े की सिलाई का कमी-ज्यादा देखने के लिए आप सोमवार को आ सकेंगे ?	Will you come on Monday for try. विल् यू कम ऑन मन्डे फॉर् ट्राइ।
Dekhūn̐. Na. Somvār ṭhīk nahīn̐ rahegā, Ma galvār ko Āūn̐ to ? देखूँ, न सोमवार ठीक नहीं रहेगा, मंगलवार का आऊँ तो ?	Let me see, I think Monday wouldbe awkward. लैट् मी सी, आय् थिंक् मडे वुड् बी आकवर्ड।

Bahut́ achchhā. Ma galvāŕ ko taiyāŕ rakh́tā hūn̈. बहुत अच्छा. मंगलवार को तैयार रखता हूँ।	Very good, sir, I shall stitch it by Tuesday. वैरी गुड्, आय शैल स्टिच इट् बॉय ट्यूस्डे।
Auŕ koī sevā (khidḿat́) ? और कोई सेवा (ख़िदमत) ?	Is there anything else I can do for you ? इज़् देअर्- एनीथिंग् एल्स् आय् कॅन् डू फॉ- यू ?
Na, auŕ kuchh́ nahīn̈. Achchhā chalen̈, Namaste. न, और कुछ नहीं. अच्छा चलें, नमस्ते.	No. I think not. Good bye नो. आय् थिंक् नॉट्. गुड्- बाय्।
Namaste, Sah́b́. नमस्ते, साहब।	Good morning, Sir. गुड् मॉर्निंग्. सर्

***At the Shoemakers*: जूते वाले की दुकान में**

1. Muze ek joḍa jūtā chāhie. मुझे एक जोड़ा जूता चाहिए।	I'd like a pair of shoes. आय् वुड् लाइक् अ पेअर्- ऑफ् शूज़्।

2. Dekh́tā hūn̐ (Main̐ pahańkaŕ dekh́tā hūn̐.)	I will try them on.
देखता हूँ (मैं पहनकर देखता हूँ)।	आय् विल् ट्राय् देम् ऑन्।
3. Ye bahut tāṇ hain̐.	These are too narrow.
ये बहुत तंग हैं।	दीज़् आर्- टू नॅरौ।
4. Iśse baḍā hai ?	Do you have larger than this ?
इससे बड़ा है ?	डू यू हैव् लार्जर् दॅन् दिस् ?
5. Muze chhoṭā chāhiye.	I want a smaller size.
मुझे छोटा चाहिये।	आय् वांट् अ स्मालर् साइज़्।
6. Panje kuchh́ chauḍe chāhiye.	I want paws a bit wider.
पंजे कुछ चौड़े चाहिये।	आय् वांट् पाज़् अ बिट् वाइडर्।
7. Yahī brāuń men̐ hai kyā ?	Do you have the same in brown ?
यही ब्राउन में है क्या ?	डू यू हैव् दसेम् इन् ब्राउन् ?

8. Eḍī bahuť uňchī hai. — The heels are too high.
एड़ी बहुत ऊँची है। — द हील्स् आ- टू हाय्।

9. Ise siye ge (sie ge) ? — Can you stich this ?
Isḱī silāī kaŕ
saḱte haiň ?
इसे सियेंगे (सिएँगे) ? — कॅन् यू स्टिच् दिस् ?
इसकी सिलाई कर
सकते हैं ?

10. Isḱī marammaṫ — Can you repair these shoes ?
kare ge?
इसकी मरम्मत — कॅन् यू रिपेअर् दीज़् शूज़् ?
करेंगे ?

11. Maiň in jūtoň meň — I want to have these shoes
naye talle aūŕ nayī — resoled and rehealed.
eḍiyāň lagānā chāhtā
hūň.
मैं इन जूतों में — आय् वांट् टु हैव् दीज़् शूज़्
नए तल्ले और नयी — रिसोल्ड् ॲण्ड् रिहील्ड्।
एड़ियाँ लगाना चाहता
हूँ।

12. Mere jūte meň kīĺ — Ther is a nail in my shoe.
nikĺī hai.

मेरे जूते में कील निकली है। — देअर्- इज़् अ नेल् इन् माय् शू।

13. Mere jūte kā nāṕ len̐. — Measure me for a pair of shoes.
मेरे जूते का नाप लें। — मेज़र् मी फा- अ पेअ- ऑफ् शूज़्।

14. Inh́en̐ jarā dhīlā banāyen̐. — Make them a bit easy.
इन्हें जरा ढीला बनायें। — मेक् देम् अ बिट् ईज़ी।

15. Ye kab́ taiyāŕ ho ge ? — When will the be ready ?
ये कब तैयार होंगे ? — व्हेन् विल् दे बी रेडी ?

16. Āṕne mere jūte durusť kiye hain̐ ? — Have you mended my shoes?
आपने मेरे जूते दुरुस्त किए हैं ? — हैव् यू मेंडेड् माय् शूज़् ?

At the Doctor's : डॉक्टर के यहाँ

1. Ḍakṭaŕ sāh́b́ hain̐ kyā ? — Is doctor in ?
डॉक्टर साहब हैं क्या ? — इज़् डॉक्टर् इन् ?

2. Rogī dekh́ne gaye hain̐. रोगी देखने गये हैं।	He has gone for a visit. ही हॅज़् गॉन´ फॉ˗ अ विज़िट्।
3. Ve kab́ āye ge ? वे कब आयेंगे ?	When would he come back ? व्हेन् वुड् ही कम् बॅक् ?
4. Baiṭhiye, abhī aye ge. बैठिये। अभी आयेंगे।	Be seated. He will be here soon. बी सीटेड्। ही विल् बी हिअ˗ सून्।
5. Namaste, dāktaŕ sāhab́. नमस्ते, डॉक्टर साहब !	Good morning, doctor ! गुड् मौर्निंग्, डॉक्टर।
6. Namaste, kāfī deŕ tak ápko baiṭhnā paḍā. नमस्ते, काफी देर तक आपको बैठना पड़ा।	Good morning, sorry, you had to wait for a long time. गुड् मौर्निंग्, सॉरी, यू हॅड् टु वेट् फॉ˗ अ लॉंग् टाइम्।
7.(Āṕko) kyā taklīf hai ? (आपको) क्या तकलीफ है ?	What's wrong with you ? व्हाट्´ज़् रॉंग् विद् यू ?
8. Muze zukāḿ auŕ būkhāŕ hai. मुझे जुकाम और बुखार है।	I am suffering from bad cough and fever. आय् ॲम् सफरिंग् फ्रॉम् बॅड् कफ् ॲण्ड् फिवर्।
9. (Āṕko) kab́ se būkhāŕ	Since when have you been

hai ?
(आपको) कब से बुखार
है ?

suffering from fever ?
सिंस् व्हेन् हैव् यू बीन्
सफरिंग् फ्राम् फिवर् ?

10. Pichhle shanivār kī rāt se.
पिछले शनिवार की रात से।

Since last Saturday night.
सिन्स् लास्ट् सटर्डे नाइट्।

11. Dekhen̐, hāth batāyen̐.
देखें, हाथ बतायें।

Well, let me feel your pulse.
वेल्, लेट् मी फील् योर्- पल्स्।

12. Muze nīnd nahīn̐ ātī.
मुझे नींद नहीं आती।

I don't get sleep.
आय् डोंट गेट् स्लीप्।

13. (Apnī) jībh dikhāyen̐.
(अपनी) जीभ दिखायें।

Show me your tongue .
शो मी योर्-र टङ्ग्।

14. Pākhānā sāf (khulkar) hotā hai ?
पाखाना साफ (खुलकर)
होता है ?

Are your bowels regular ?
आर्- योर्- बॉवेल्स् रेगुलर् ?

15. Pichhle do din se ek bār bhī nahīn̐ huī.
पिछले दो दिन से एक बार
भी नहीं हुई।

Not even once in the last two days.
नॉट् इवन् वन्स् इन् द लास्ट् टू
डेज़्।

16. Khansī ātī hai ?
खाँसी आती है ?
Do you cough ?
डू यू कॉफ् ?

17. kabhī-kabhī.
कभी-कभी।
Sometimes.
समटाइम्स्।

18. Iś paŕ leṭ jāyen.
इस पर लेट जायें।
Lie down on the bed.
लार्य डॉउन् ऑन् द बेड्।

19. Dukhtā hai ?
दुखता है ?
Does that pain you ?
डज् दॅट् पेन् यू ?

20. Thoḍā-thoḍā.
थोड़ा- थोड़ा।
A little.
अ लिटर्ल्।

21. Dekho, main abhī ek injeksaṅ detā hūn.
देखो, मैं अभी एक इंजेक्शन देता हूँ।
Now, I am giving an injection.
नाऊ, आय् अम् गिविंग् ॲन् इन्जेक्शन्।

22. Yah davāī do dinon ke lie hai.
यह दवाई दो दिनों के लिए है।
This medicine is for two days.
दिस् मेडिसर्न इज़् फॉ- टू डेज़्।

23. Har chār ghaṇṭe ke bād ek khurāk len.	Take a dose every four hour.
हर चार घंटे के बाद एक खुराक लें।	टेक् अ डोज़ एव्री फोर् अवर्।
24. Yah goli sote samay len.	Take this pill at bed time.
यह गोली सोते समय लें।	टेक् दिस् पिल् ॲट् बेड् टाइम्।
25. Chup chāp bistare par paḍe rahen.	Lie down on bed quitely.
चुपचाप बिस्तरे पर पड़े रहें।	लाय डाउन् ऑन् बेड् क्वायेट्ली।
26. Sirph chāy, kāfī biskit len.	Take only Tea, coffee and biscuits.
सिर्फ चाय, कॉफी बिस्किट लें।	टेक् ऑन्ली टी, कॉफी ॲण्ड बिस्क्टि्स्.

Asking the way : रास्ता पूछना

1. Māf kījiye Steṣan kā rāstā batāye ge ?	Excuse me, can you tell me the way to the Station ?

माफ कीजिये, स्टेशन का रास्ता बतायेंगे ?

एक्स्क्यूज़्मी, कॅन यू टेल् मी दॅ वे टु दॅ स्टेशन् ?

2. kaun̐-sā Steṣan ?
कौन-सा स्टेशन ?

Which Station ?
व्हिच् स्टेशन् ?

3. Is ṭwiń-siṭī men̐ tīń railve-steṣań hain̐.
इस टिव्न-सिटी में तीन रेलवे-स्टेशन हैं ।

There are three Railway Stations in this Twin-city.
देअॅ- आॅ- थ्री रेलवे स्टेशन्स इन् दिस् ट्विन सिटी ।

4. Merā matlab - sikandrābād railve steṣań.
मेरा मतलब-सिकंदराबाद रेल्वे स्टेशन ।

I mean the Secunderabad Rly. Station.
आय् मीन् दॅ सिकंदराबाद रेल्वे स्टेशन ।

5. Oh ! Vah thoḍā dūŕ hai.
ओह ! वह थोड़ा दूर है ।

Oh ! That's rather a long way
ओहॅ ! दॅट्ज़् रादर् अ लाॅंग वे ।

6. Kitnā dūŕ ?
कितना दूर ?

How far it is from here ?
हाउ फॉ- इट् इज़् फ्रॉम् हिअॅ- ?

7. Karībań ek mīl.
करीबन् एक मील ।

About a mile.
अबॉउट् अ माइलॅ ।

8. Kiś rāste ? किस रास्ते ?	Which way is it ? व्हिच् वे इज़् इट् ?
9. Sīdhe jā-i-ye. सीधे जाइये ।	Go straight ahead. गो स्ट्रेट् अहेड्।
10. Tīśre chauk paŕ jā-i-ye. तीसरे चौक पर जाइये ।	Go to the third cross-roads. गो टु द थर्ड् क्रॉस रोड्स ।
11. Auŕ vahān̐ ṭrāfic la-iť ke dāyen̐ muḍiye. और वहाँ ट्राफिक लाइट के दायें मुड़िये।	And turn right at the traffic light. ॲण्ड् टर्न् राइट् ॲट् द ट्राफिक लाइट ।
12. Vaħ rāstā Sikandrābād steṣań jātā hai. वह रास्ता सिकंदराबाद स्टेशन जाता है ।	That road leads to the Secunderabad Station. दॅट् रोड् लीड्स टु द सिकंदराबाद स्टेशन।
13. Dhanyavād Āpkā bahut-bahut dhanyavād. धन्यवाद ! आपका बहुत-बहुत धन्यवाद !	Thank you, very much. थैंक् यू वेरी मच् ।

14. Kaṭaī jarūrat nahīn̐. — Not at all.

कतई जरूरत नहीं। — नॉट् अॅट् ऑल।

Railway-Journey : रेल यात्रा

Reservation of Berth : आरक्षण

1. Mīnār expres kā rizarveshan milegā kyā ? — Can I get a reservation on the Minar Express ?

मीनार एक्सप्रेस का रिझर्वेशन मिलेगा क्या ? — कॅन् आय् गेट् अ रिझर्वेशन ऑन् दॅ मीनार एक्सप्रेस ?

2. Kis darje kā ? — What Class ?

किस दर्जे का ? — व्हॉट् क्लास ?

3. Dūsre darje ka — The second class

दूसरे दर्जे का। — दॅ सेकंड् क्लास्।

4. Hān̐, milegā. — Certainly.

हाँ, मिलेगा। — सरटेन्ली।

5. Kab jānā hai ? — When do you want to go ?

कब जाना है ? — व्हेन् डू यू वांट् टु गो ?

6. Panch tārīkh ko. पाँच तारीख को ।	On the fifth. ऑन् दॅ फिफ्थ् ।
7. Āṭh tārīkh tak ke Sabhi- ṭikaṭ bik chuke hain. आठ तारीख तक के सभी टिकट बिक चुके हैं ।	Sorry, All seats are booked upto the eighth. सॉरी, ऑल सीट्स् आर्- बुक्ड् अपटु दॅ एट्थ् ।
8. Nau tārīkh kā ṭikaṭ dījiye. नौ तारीख का टिकट दीजिये ।	Book me for the ninth. बुक् मी फॉर्- दॅ नाइन्थ् ।
9. Kitne ṭikaṭ chāhiye ? कितने टिकट चाहिये ?	How many ? हाउ मेनी ?
10. Sirph ek. सिर्फ एक ।	Just one. जस्ट् वन ।
11. Abhī ṭikaṭ le ge kyā ? अभी टिकट लेंगे क्या ?	Will you have it just now ? विल् यू हॅव इट् जस्ट् नाउ?
12. Hān, abhī. हाँ, अभी ।	Yes, just now. यस, जस्ट् नाउ ।

In the Train : ट्रेन में

13. Kyā Mīnār Express	Does the Minar Express leave

samaý paŕ chhūṭegī. क्या मीनार एक्सप्रेस समय पर छूटेगी ?	in time ? डज़् द॑ मीनार एकस्प्रेस् लीव॑ इन् टाइम॑ ?
14. Han̐, vaĥ samaý paŕ chhūṭegī. हाँ, वह समय पर छूटेगी ।	Yes, it will leave in time. यस्, इट् विल् लीव् इन् टाइम् ।
15. Magaŕ dekhen̐, nayī samaý sāriṇī kal hī āyī hai. मगर देखें, नयी समय-सारिणी कल ही आयी है।	But, let us see, the new time - table came into operation just yesterday. बट्, लेट् अस् सी, द॑ न्यू टाइम- टेबल केम् इन्टु ऑपरेशन जस्ट् यस्टरडे् ।
16. Samaý men̐ ko-ī parivartań to nahīn̐ hai ? समय में कोई परिवर्तन तो नहीं है ?	Is there any change in time ? इज़् देअ॑ एनि चेंज़् इन् टाइम् ?
17. Nahīn̐, ko-ī parivartań nahīn̐. नहीं, कोई परिवर्तन नहीं ।	No, there is no change in time. नो, देअ॑ इज़् नो चेंज़् इन् टाइम् ।

18. Gāḍī kiś platfārḿ paŕ āyegī ?
गाड़ी किस प्लेटफार्म पर आयेगी ?

On which platform will the train be coming ?
आन विच प्लॅटफ़ॉर्म विल् दॅ ट्रेन् बी कमिंग् ?

19. Do naṁbaŕ paŕ.
दो नंबर पर ।

On number two.
ऑन् नंबर् टु ।

20. Ai kulī, sāmāń uṭhā-o; naṁbeŕ kyā hai ?
ऐ कुली, सामान उठाओ; नंबर क्या है ?

Porter, take the luggage; what's the number ?
पोर्टर्, टेक् दॅ लगेज़्
व्हाट्ज़् दॅ नंबर ?

21. Āṕko kahāँ jānā hai ?
आपको कहाँ जाना है ?

Where are you going ?
व्हेअर्- आर्- यू गोइंग् ?

22. Baṁba-ī
बंबई ।

Bombay.
बॉम्बे ।

23. Gāḍī Baṁba-ī kai baje pahuँchegī ?
गाड़ी बंबई कै बजे पहुँचेगी ?

When will the train reach Bombay ?
व्हेन् विल् दॅ ट्रेन् रीच् बॉम्बे ?

24. Baḍi subaḣ (taḍke) chāŕ baje.

At four early in the morning.

बड़ी सुबह (तड़के) चार बजे ।	अॅट् फोर्- अर्ली इन् द मोर्निंग् ।

Alighting from the Train : ट्रेन से उतरना

25. E kulī, ए कुली,	I say, Porter. आय् से, पोर्टर् ।
26. Āyā Sāhb ! आया साहब !	Coming sir ! कमिंग् सर् !
27. Kyā hukm hai, sāhab ! क्या हुक्म है, साहब !	Yes, Sir ! यस्, सर् !
28. Mera sāmān uṭhā-o. मेरा सामान उठाओ ।	Remove the luggage. रिमुव द लगेज़् ।
29. Ve do sūtkesa aur yah surāhı. वे दो सूटकेस और यह सुराही ।	Those two suit-cases and this surahi. दोज़् टू सूटकेसिज़ अॅण्ड दिस् सुराही ।
30. Tumhārā nambar kyā hai? तुम्हारा नंबर क्या है ?	What's your number ? व्हाट्स यों- नंबर ?
31. Taxi stand le chalo.	Take me to the taxi-stand.

टैक्सी-स्टैण्ड ले चलो ।	टेक् मी टु द टॅक्सी-स्टॅण्ड् .
32. Kit́ne paise dene hain̐ ?	How muzch to pay ?
कितने पैसे देने हैं ?	हाउ मच् टु पे ?
33. Ye lo paise.	Have this money ?
ये लो पैसे ।	हैव दिस मनी।
34. Sabhī aṕne li-e rakho.	Keep it all for you.
सभी अपने लिए रखो ।	कीप् इट् ऑल् फॉ- यू।
35. Sāhab́, āṕkā main̐ atyant ābhārī hūn̐ !	Thank you so much, Sir !
साहब, आपका मैं अत्यंत आभारी हूँ ।	थैंक् यू सो मच्, सर् !

By Bus : बस से

1. Bas stand kahān̐ hai ?	Where is the bus stand ?
बस स्टैण्ड कहाँ है ?	व्हेअ- इज़् द बस् स्टैण्ड ?
2. Inqvāyarī Ăphiś kahān̐ hai ?	Where is the Inquiry office ?
इन्क्वायरी ऑफिस कहाँ है ?	व्हेअ- इज़् द इन्क्वायरी ऑफिस ?
3. Chāŕ Mināŕ ke li-e basen̐	Which can we get a bus to

kahān̐ milen̐gī ?
चार मिनार के लिए बसें
कहाँ मिलेंगी ?

Char Minar ?
विच - कॅन् वी गेट् अ बस् टु
चार मीनार?

4. Kiś naṁbar kī baś
Chāŕ Mīnāŕ jātī hai ?
किस नंबर की बस
चार मीनार जाती है ?

What number is to Char
Minar ?
व्हाट् नंबर इज़् टु चार मीनार ?

5. Chāŕ Mīnāŕ ke li-e vāyā
Sālār Jung Muziyam
kauń sī baś hai ?
चार मीनार के लिए वाया
सालार जंग म्युज़ियम
कौन सी बस है ?

What bus do I take to Char
Minar via Sālār Jung
Museum ?
व्हाट् बस् डू आय् टेक टु चार
मीनार वाया सालार जंग म्युजियम?

6. Agalī baś kab́ hai ?
अगली बस कब है ?

When is the next bus ?
व्हेन् इज़् दं नेक्स्ट् बस् ?

7. Baś kahīn̐ badalnī hogī ?
बस कहीं बदलनी होगी ?

Where do we have to change
bus ?
ह्वेयर डू वी हैव् टु चेंज़् दि बस ?

8. Kitnā vakṭ letī hai ?
कितना वक्त लेती है

How long does it take to Char
Minar ?
हाउ लाँग् डज़् इट् टेक् टु चार

मिनार ?

9. Kandaktar, yah' baś Chāŕ Mīnāŕ jātī hai kyā?
कंडक्टर, यह बस
चार मीनार जाती है क्या ?

Conductor, does this bus go to Char Minar ?
कंडक्टर, डज़् दिस् बस् गो
टु चार मीनार ?

10. Jī, magar yah' Kāchīgudā hokaŕ jātī hai.
जी, मगर यह काचीगुडा
होकर जाती है ।

Yes sir, it does, but goes via Kacheguda.
यस् सर्, इट् डज़्, बट् ग़ोज वाया
काचीगुडा।

11. Ko-ī bāt́ nahīn̐.
कोई बात नहीं ।

Oh! That doesn't matter.
ओ ! दॅट् डज़न्ट् मॅटर ।

12. A dar ā-e-ye, Sāhab !
अंदर आइये, साहब !

Get in please, Sir.
गेट् इन् प्लीज़्, सर ।

13. Dhanyavād́
धन्यवाद ।

Thank you.
थैंक यू ।

14. Char Minar ke li-e chār ṭiket́ chāhi-e.
चार मीनार के लिए
चार टिकट चाहिए।

I want four tickets to Char Minar.
आय् वांट् फॉ- टिकेट्स टु चार
मीनार्।

15. Do ful auŕ do hāph.

Two full and two half.

दो फुल ऑर दो हाफ् ।	टु फुल् ॲण्ड् टु हाफ् ।
16. Kyā kirāyā hai ?	How much is the fare to Char Minar ?
क्या किराया है ?	हाउ मच् इज़् दॅ फेअॅ- टु चार मीनार ?
17. Bach-choṅ kā ādhā ṭikaṭ hai ?	Is it half ticket for a child ?
बच्चों का आधा टिकट है ?	इज़् इट् हाफ् टिकट् फॉ- अ चाइल्ड् ?
18. Yaḣ 10 Sāl kā hai auŕ yaḣ 12 kī .	He is 10 and she is 12 .
यह 10 साल का है और यह 12 की ।	ही इज़् टेन् ॲण्ड् शी इज़् ट्वेल्व ।
19. ko-ī baiṭhā hai ?	Is this seat vacant ?
कोई बैठा है ?	इज़् दिस् सीट् वेकेन्ट ?
20. Jagaḣ khālī hai ?	Is that seat free ?
जगह खाली है ?	इज़् दॅट् सीट् फ्री ?
21. Ho na ho, yaḣ merī sīṭ hai.	I think that's my seat.
हो न हो, यह मेरी सीट् है ।	आय् थिंक् दॅट्'स माय् सीट् ।
22. Chār Mīnāŕ ke li-e kitnā	How much time will it take to

vakt legī ?

चार मीनार के लिए कितना वक्त लेगी ?

Char Minar ?

हाउ मच् टाइम् विल् इट् टेक टु चार मीनार ?

23. Haḿ Chāŕ Mīnāŕ kab́ pahun̈che ge ?

हम चार मीनार कब पहुँचेंगे ?

Can you tell me when we get to Char Minar ?

कॅन् यू टेल् मी व्हेन वी गेट् टु चार मीनार ?

24. Yah́ kon-sā stăṕ hai ?

यह कौन-सा स्टॉप है ?

What stop is this ?

व्हाट् स्टॉप् इज़् दिस् ?

25. Kahe ge, kab́ utaŕnā hai ?

कहेंगे, कब उतरना है ?

Will you tell me, when to get off ?

विल् यू टेल् मी, व्हेन् टु गेट् ऑफ् ?

26. Hamen̈ Chāŕ Mīnāŕ utaŕnā hai.

हमें चार मीनार उतरना है ।

We want to get off at Char Minar.

वी वांट् टु गेट् औफ् अॅट् चार मीनार ।

27. Agle stăp paŕ utaŕnā hai.

अगले स्टॉप् पर उतरना है ।

Please let us off at the next stop.

प्लीज़् लेट् अस् ऑफ् अॅट् दॅ नेक्स्ट स्टॉप् ।

By Taxi : टैक्सी से

1. Kṛipyā ek taxī bulāye / ma gāye .
कृपया एक टॅक्सी बुलायें/ मँगायें ।

Get me a taxi, please.
गेट् मी अ टॅक्सी, प्लीज़् ।

2. Svapna-sarovaŕ le chalo.
स्पप्न-सरोवर ले चलो ।

Take me to Svapna-sarovar .
टेक् मी टु स्वप्न-सरोवर ।

3. Svapna-Sarovaŕ yahān̐ se kitnī dūŕ hai ?
स्वप्न-सरोवर यहाँ से कितनी दूर है ।

How far is it to Svapna-sarovar?
हाउ फॉ- इज़् इट् टु स्वप्न-सरोवर?

4. Agale moḍ paŕ bāyen̐/ dāyen̐ muḍo.
अगले मोड़ पर बायें/ दायें मुड़ो।

Turn left/right at the next corner.
टर्न् लेफ्ट्/ राइट् अॅट् द नेक्स्ट् कॉर्नर्।

5. Bilkul sīdhe chalo.
बिलकुल सीधे चलो

Go straight ahead.
गो स्ट्रेट् अहेड् ।

6. Itnī raftār se mat chalā-o.	Don't drive so fast.
इतनी रफ्तार से मत चलाओ ।	डोंट् ड्राइव सो फास्ट् ।
7. Thoḍā aur slo chalā-o.	Could you drive more slowly ?
थोड़ा और स्लो चलाओ ।	कुड् यू ड्राइव् मोर् स्लोव्ली ?
8. Āp phik a na karen, sāhab.	Don't worry, sir.
आप फिक्र न करें, साहब ।	डोंट् वरी, सर् ।
9. Main siddhahast hūn. Merā hāth saph hai.	I am an expert.
मैं सिद्धहस्त हूँ । मेरा हाथ साफ है ।	आय् ॲम् ॲन् एक्सपर्ट ।
10. vah imārat kaisī hai drāivar ?	What building is that, driver ?
वह इमारत कैसी है, ड्राइवर !	व्हाट् बिल्डिंग् इज् ॅट्, ड्राइवर !
11. Kabhi vah rājā kā mahal thā.	Once that was the king's palace.
कभी वह राजा का महल था ।	वन्स ॅट् वाज़् दं किंग्स् पैलेस् ।

12. Aj vah yunivarsitī hai.
आज वह यूनिवर्सिटी है ।

Now, that's the University.
नाउ, दॅट्'स द यूनिवर्सिटी ।

13. Yahān̐ rokūn̐ kyā ?
यहाँ रोकूँ क्या ?

Shall I stop here ?
शल् आय् स्टॉप् हिअ- ?

14. Ek nazar se prasiddha rājmahal dekhne ke li-e.
एक नज़र से प्रसिद्ध राजमहल देखने के लिए ।

To have a look at the famous palace.
टु हैव् अ लुक् ॲट् द फेमस् पॅलेस ।

15. Abhī nahīn̐, pahle hotal chalo.

अभी नहीं, पहले होटल चलो ।

Not now, first let us go to the hotel.

नॉट् नाउ, फर्स्ट् लेट अस गो टु द होटल् ।

16. Bahut achchhā, Sāhab !
बहुत अच्छा, साहब !

All right, Sir !
ऑल राइट्, सर् !

17. Ab ham Svapna-sarovar men̐ praves kar rahe hain̐, Sāhab.
अब हम स्वप्न-सरोवर

We are now entering in the Svapna-sarovar, Sir.

वी आ- नाउ एंटरिंग् इन्

में प्रवेश कर रहे
हैं, साहब।

दर्स्वप्न सरोवर, सर् ।

18. Accha ! Mujhe pata
nahiñ tha ki itne pas hai.
अच्छा ! मुझे पता नहीं था कि
इतने पास है।

Are we ? I never knew
it was so near.
आर्- वुइ ? आय् नेवर्- न्यू इट्
वाज् सो निअर्- ।

19. Ý achchhā hai kyā ?
य' अच्छा है क्या ?

Is it a good one ?
इज् इट् अ गुड् वन् ?

20. Bilā shaḱ, Sahab́, ý
bahut́ hī āle darje kā hai.
बिला शक, साहब; य'
बहुत ही आले दर्जे का है ।

Certainly, Sir, It is very posh.
सर्टेन्ली, सर्, इट् इज़ व्हेरी पॉश .

21. Roko yahā̃n.
रोको यहाँ ।
Mujhe is pate par Dharm
shala / Gurudwara /
Hotel le chalo.
मुझे इस पते पर / धर्म-
शाला/गुरुद्वारा/
होटल ले चलो।

Stop here, please.
स्टॉप् हिअर्-, प्लीज़् ।
Take me to/ this address/
Hotel/ Gurudvārā
Dharamshala
टेक् मी टु दिस एड्रेस
होटल, गुरुद्वारा,
धर्मशाला।

22. Bag uṭhāne men meri madad kare ge ?
बैग उठाने में मेरी मदद करेंगे ?

Could you help to carry my bags ?
कुड् यू हेल्प् टु कॅरी माय् बॅग्स् ?

23. Main jarā jaldī men hūn.
मैं जरा जल्दी में हूँ ।

I'm in a hurry.
आर्य् म् इन् अ हरी ।

24. Kitne paise ?
कितने पैसे ?

How much ?
हाउ मच् ?

25. Ye lo.
ये लो ।

Take this.
टेक दिस।

26. Bākī paise ye rahe, Sāhab.
बाकी पैसे ये रहे, साहब ।

Here's the change, Sir.
हिअर्- ज़ दं चेंज्, सर् ।

27. Yah tumhāre li-e hī.
यह तुम्हारे लिए ही ।

Keep it for you.
कीप् इट् फॉर् यू ।

28. Apkī baḍi meharbānī, Sāhab.
आपकी बड़ी मेहरबानी, साहब ।

So kind of you, sir,
सो काइंड् ऑफ् यू, सर् ।

29. Dhanyavād, Sāhab́.	Thank you, Sir.
धन्यवाद, साहब ।	थैंक् यू, सर्।

By Steamer-boat : स्टीमर-बोट से

1. Havā joŕ se bah́ rahī hai.	It is very windy.
हवा जोर से बह रही है ।	इट् इज़् वेरि विंडी ।
2. Samudŕ tūphāni hai.	The sea is rough.
समुद्र तूफानी है ।	द॔ सी इज़् रफ् ।
3. Nāv' kahān̐ hai ?	Where is the boat ?
नाव कहाँ है ?	व्हेअ॔ इज़् द॔ बोट् ?
4. Nāv' dūb́ rahī hai.	The boat is sinking.
नाव डूब रही है ।	द॔ बोट् इज़् सिंकिंग् ।
5. Mān̐zhī kahān̐ hai ?	Where is the crew ?
माँझी कहाँ है ?	व्हेअ॔ इज़् द॔ क्रयू ?
6. Vah́ nāv' chhodḣkar bhāǵ gayā.	He left the boat and ran away.
वह नाव छोड़कर	ही लेफ्ट् द॔ बोट् ॲण्ड् रन् अवे ।

भाग गया ।

7. Āj́ samud shānt́ hai. आज समुद्र शांत है ।

To-day, the sea is calm. टु–डे, द´ सी इज़् काम् ।

8. Yah ach-chhī nāv' hai. यह अच्छी नाव है ।

This is a good boat. दिस् इज़् अ गुड् बोट ।

9. Iśmen̐ kitne yatrī hain̐ ? इसमें कितने यात्री हैं ।

How many passengers are there ? हाउ मेनि पॅसेंजर्स् आ´–देअ´ ?

10. Muze mālūḿ nahīn̐. मुझे मालूम नहीं ।

I donot know आय् डु नॉट नो।

11. Āṕ jahāj́ dekh́ sakte hain̐? आप जहाज़ देख सकते हैं ?

Can you see the steamer ? कॅन् यू सी द´स्टीमर् ?

12. Duśrā jahāj kab́ ravānā hogā ? दूसरा जहाज़ कब रवाना होगा ?

When does the next steamer starts ? व्हेन् डज़् द´ नेक्स्ट् स्टीमर् स्टार्ट्स् ?

13. Yahān̐ se Eliphanṭā taḱ jāne ko sṭimar

Is there a steamer-boat running from here to

milĺ saḱtā hai ? यहाँ से एलिफण्टा तक जाने को स्टीमर मिल सकता है ?	Elephanta? इज़् देअ॑अ स्टीमर्-बोट् रनिंग् फ्रॉम हिअ॑- टु एलिफॅण्टा ।
14. Dińmen̐ kit́nī bāŕ ? दिन में कितनी बार ?	How many times a day ? हाउ मेनि टाइम्स अ डे ?
15. Bhāḍā kyā hai ? भाड़ा क्या है ?	What is the fare ? व्हाट् इज द॑ फेअ॑- ?
16. Khāne ko kuchh́ milegā ? खाने को कुछ मिलेगा ?	Can I get something to eat ? कॅन् आय् गेट् समथिंग् टु ईट् ?

To open an Account in a Bank : बैंक में खाता खोलना

1. Kyā main̐ andaŕ āsakata hūn ? क्या मैं अंदर आ सकता हूँ ?	May I come in ? मे आय् कम्॑ इन् ?
2. Avaśya. अवश्य ।	Certainly. सर्टेन्लि ।
3. Baiṭhiye. बैठिये ।	Take your seat, please. टेक्॑ यॉ॑ सीट्, प्लीज़् ।

4. Dhanyavād . धन्यवाद ।	Thanks . थैंक्स् ।
5. Kahiye, kyā āj ā hai ? कहिये, क्या आज्ञा है ?	What can I do for you ? व्हाट् कॅन् आय् डू फॉ यू ?
6. Main̐ āpke bank men̐ khātā kholnā chāhtā hūn̐. मैं आपके बैंक में खाता खोलना चाहता हूँ ।	I want to open an account in your bank. आय् वांट् टु ओपन् ॲन अकॉउंट इन यों बैंक।
7. Āpkā saharṣ svāgat hai, Sāhab ! आपका सहर्ष स्वागत है, साहब ।	You are warmly welcomed, Sir ! यू आर्- वार्म्लि बेल्कम्ड्, सर् ।
Hamen̐ āpkī sevā karne kā maukā den̐. हमें आपकी सेवा करने का मौका दें ।	Give us an opportunity of your service. गिव्ह् अस् ॲन् ऑपरचुनिटि ऑफ यों सर्व्हिस् ।
8. Kis tarah kā khātā kholnā chāhte hain̐ ? किस तरह का खाता खोलना चाहते हैं ?	Which type of account do you want to open ? व्हिच् टाइप् ऑफ् अकॉउंट् डू यू वांट् टु ओपन् ?
9. Sa chay (bachat) khātā.	A Savings Bank Account.

संचय (बचत) खाता ।	अ सेव्हिंग् बैड्क् अकॉउंट् ।
10. Nijī yā sanyukt ? निजी या संयुक्त ?	A personal or joint account ? अ परसनल् ऑ' जॉइंट् अकॉउंट् ?
11. Nijī, Sāhab. निजी, साहब !	Personal, Please. परसनल्, प्लीज़् ।
12. Yah rahā farm ise bhariye aur ek ai-se vyakti se sahī len jiskā is bank men khātā ho.	Here's the form, fill it up, and get it introduced by a person who has his account in this bank.
यह रहा फार्म इसे भरिये और एक ऐसे वयक्ति से सही लें जिसका इस बैड्क में खाता हो ।	हिअ॑-ज़् द॑ फॉर्म्, फिल् इट् अप्, ॲण्ड् गेट् इट् इन्ट्रॉड्यूस्ड बाय् अ परसन् व्हू हॅज् हिज़् अकॉउंट इन दिस् बॅड्क् ।
13. Dhanyavād. धन्यवाद ।	Thank you. थैक् यू ।

Withdrawal of the Money : बैंक से पैसा निकालना

1. Kripya viḍrāal fārm den.	(Please), give me a withdrawal form.
कृपया विड्राअल फॉर्म दें ।	प्लीज्, गिव् मी अ विद्ड्राअल् फॉर्म् ।

2. Pass-Book lāye hain̐ kyā ?	Have you brought your Pass-Book ?
पास बुक लाये हैं क्या ?	हैव् यू ब्रॉट् यॉ-र् पास-बुक् ?
3. Jī hān̐, yé rahiā pās-buk.	Yes Sir, here's my Pass-Book.
जी हाँ, य रहा पास-बुक ।	यस् सर्, हिअ-ज़् माय् पास-बुक् ।
4. Yah tokań lījiye.	Take this Token, please.
यह टोकन लीजिये ।	टेक् दिस् टोकन्, प्लीज़् ।
5. Paise agalī khiḍkī par milenge.	You will get the money at the next window.
पैसे अगली खिड़की पर मिलेंगे ।	यू विल् गेट् द मनि अॅट् द नेक्स्ट् विंडो ।
6. Thoḍī der baiṭhiye.	(Please), Be seated for a while.
थोड़ी देर बैठिये ।	(प्लीज़्) बी सीटेड् फॉ- अ व्हाइल् ।
7. Namber pachī .	Twenty-five number, please.
नंबर पचीस ।	ट्वेन्टि-फाइव नंबर, प्लीज़् ।
8. Hān̐ jī.	Yes, Sir.
हाँ जी ।	यस्, सर ।

9. Tokań den̐.	Give me the token, please.
टोकन दें ।	गिव् मी द´टोकन, प्लीज़् ।
10. Kyā āṕ sau-sau rupýe ke note lenā chāhe ge ?	Would you like to have hundred rupees notes ?
क्या आप सौ-सौ रुपये के नोट लेना चाहेंगे ?	वुड् यू लाइक् टु हैव् हड्रेड् रुपीज़् नॉट्स् ।
11. Chalega.	Will do.
चलेगा ।	विल् डू ।
12. Dhanyavāḍ.	Thank you.
धन्यवाद ।	थैंक् यू ।

Deposit of Money in the Bank : बैंक में पैसे भरना

Paise jamā kańe hain̐.	I want to deposit some money.
पैसे जमा करने हैं ।	आय् वांट् टु डिपॉसिट् सम् मनि ।
Vaḣ fārm lījiye auŕ bhaŕkaŕ dījiye.	(Please), Take that form and fill it up.
वह फॉर्म लीजिये और भरकर दीजिये ।	(प्लीज़्) टेक् दैट् फॉर्म ॲण्ड फिल् इट् अप् ।

Yah̐ fārm auŕ ye paise lījiye.	Take this form and the money, please.
यह फ़ॉर्म और ये पैसे लीजिये ।	टेक् दिस् फ़ॉर्म् ॲण्ड् द मनि, प्लीज़ ।

Yahāṅ likheṅ ki -– Kiske nam̐ yah̐ rakam̐ jamā kaŕnī hai.	Please write here– On whose name the amount is to be credited to
यहाँ लिखें कि– किसके नाम यह रकम जमा करनी है ।	प्लीज़ राइट् हिअॅ– ऑन् व्हूज़ नेम् द अमाउंट इज़ टु बी क्रेडिटेड् टु ।

Dhanyavād̐ .	Thanks.
धन्यवाद ।	थैंक्स ।

यह रसीद लीजिये ।	Take this receipt, please.
Yah̐ rasīd̐ lījiye.	टेक् दिस् रिसीट्, प्लीज़ ।

Crediting the Cheque in the Bank : बैंक में चेक जमा करना

Maiṅ is chek̐ ko apne khāte meṅ jamā kaŕnā chāhtā hūṅ.	I want to credit this cheque to my account.

मैं इस चेक को अपने खाते में जमा करना चाहता हूँ ।	आय् वांट् टु क्रेडिट् दिस् चेक् टु माय् अकॉउंट् ।
Muze kahān̆ dasťkhat kaŕne chāhiye ?	Where should I sign ?
मुझे कहाँ दस्तखत करने चाहियें ?	व्हेअर्- शुड् आय् साइन् ?

Encashment of the Cheque : चेक का भुगतान

Muze iś chek ka bhugťāń chāhiye.	I want to realize this cheque, please.
मुझे इस चेक का भुगतान चाहिये।	आय् वांट् टु रिअलाइज़् दिस् चेक् प्लीज़् ।
Kripyā chek ke pīchhe hastākṣaŕ karen̆.	Will you please sign behind the cheque ?
कृपया चेक के पीछे हस्ताक्षर करें ।	विल् यू प्लीज़् साइन् बिहाइंड् द चेक ?
Yá lījiye tokań nambar 52.	Here's token No. 52.
येँ लीजिये टोकन नं० 52 ।	हिअर्-इज़् टोकन् नं० 52 ।
Dhanyavād.	Thank you.

धन्यवाद ।	थैंक् यू ।

Loan from a Bank : बैंक से कर्ज

Muze mainejaŕ se milnā hai.	I would like to see the manager.
मुझे मैनेजर से मिलना है ।	आय् वुड् लाइक् टु सी द् मैनेजर् ।
Sāmne vāle kamre men̐ jāyiye.	Go to the room over there.
सामने वाले कमरे में जाइये ।	गो टु द् रूम् ओवर्- देअर्-
Kyā main̐ andaŕ ā saktā hūn̐ ?	May I come in ?
क्या मैं अंदर आ सकता हूँ ?	मे आय् कम् इन् ?
Kahiye, ham kyā madad karen̐ ?	Tell us, what we can do for you ?
कहिये, हम क्या मदद करें ?	टेल् अस्, व्हाट् वी कॅन् डू फॉर्- यू ?

Muze thoḍā karja milega kyā ?	Can I get a small loan ?
मुझे थोड़ा कर्ज मिलेगा क्या ?	कॅन् आय् गेट् अ स्माल् लोन् ?
Sone ke gah́ne giŕvī rakh́ne paŕ milega.	You can get it aganist pledging of gold ornaments.
सोने के गहने गिरवी रखने पर मिलेगा ।	यू कॅन् गेट् इट् अगेंस्ट् प्लेजिंग् ऑफ गोल्ड् ऑनमिंट्स् ।
Byāj́ kī daŕ kyā hai ?	What is the rate of interest ?
ब्याज की दर क्या है ?	व्हाट् इज़् द रेट् ऑफ् इंटेरेस्ट् ?
Nau pratiṣat́ .	Nine per cent.
नौ प्रतिशत ।	नाइन पर सेंट् ।
Achchhā jī, dhanyavād́.	Thank you, so much, sir.
अच्छा जी, धन्यवाद ।	थैंक् यू सो मच्, सर् ।

At the Post - Office : डाक–घर में

In the cities of India, the post offices are generally opened from 10.00 am to 4.00 p.m., except Sundays. They remain closed on all Govenment holidays.

डाक-घर	ḍāḱ-ghar	Post-Office	पोस्ट्-ऑफिस
डाक का दिन	ḍāḱ kā diń	Mail-day	मेल-डे
डाक-टिकट	ḍāḱ-ṭiket	Postage-stamp	पोस्टेज-स्टैम्प
लिफाफा	liphāphā	Envelope	एन्वेलप्
अंतर्देशीय-पत्र	anterdesīya-patra	Inland-letter	इन्लैण्ड-लेटर्
पोस्ट-कार्ड	posṭ-kārd	Post-Card	पोस्ट-कार्ड
मनि-आर्डर्	mani-arḍaŕ	Money-Order	मनि-ऑर्डर्
पत्र	pat a	Letter	लेटर्
वितरण	vitaraṅ	Delivery	डिलिवरी
हवाई-डाक	havāī-ḍāḱ	Air-mail	एअर्-मेल्
पंजीकरण	panjīkaraṇ	Registration	रजिस्ट्रेशन
पंजीकृत-पत्र	panjīkrit-pat a	Registered letter	रजिस्टर्ड लेटर
पार्सल्	pārsal	Parcel	पार्सल्
पहुँच-रसीद	Pahuńch-rasīd	Acknowled-gement	एक्नॉलिज-मेंट
डाकिया	Dākiyā	Post-man	पोस्टमैन

1. Kyā āj post ăfiś khulā hai ?
   क्या आज पोस्ट ऑफिस खुला है ?

   Is the Post-Office open, to-day ?
   इज़् द् पोस्ट ऑफिस ओपन टु-डे ?

2. Hān̐, Āj́ dāk kā diń hai
हाँ, आज डाक का दिन है ।

Yes, to-day is mail-day.
यस्, टु-डे इज़् मेल्-डे ।

3. Yahān̐ se posṭ ăfiś kiṭnī dūŕ hai ?
यहाँ से पोस्ट ऑफिस कितनी दूर है ?

How far is the post-office from here !
हाउ फार् इज़् दर् पोस्ट ऑफिस फ्रॉम हिअर्- ?

4. Pān̐ch minaṭ kā rāstā hai.
पाँच मिनट का रास्ता है ।

About five minutes walk.
अबाउट् फाइव्ह मिनट्स् वाक् ।

5. Agle moḍ tak jākaŕ bāen̆ muḍ jā-i-ye.
अगले मोड़ तक जाकर बाएँ मुड़ जाइये !

Go to the next corner and turn left.
गो टु दर् नेक्सट् कॉर्नर् अण्ड् टर्न लेफ्ट ।

6. Sāhab́, kripayā yah batāiye ki iśke liye kitnā postej lagegā ?
साहब, कृपया यह बताइये कि इसके लिए कितना पोस्टेज लगेगा ।

Sir, please tell me, the postage it requires ?
सर्, प्लीज़् टेल् मी, द पोस्टेज इट् रिक्वाअर्स् ?

7. Kyā yah rajistrī-pat a hai ?
क्या यह रजिस्ट्री-पत्र है ?

Is it a registered-letter ?
इज़् इट् अ रजिस्टर्ड-लेटर् ?

8. Jī hān̐, yah rajistrī-pat a hai.
जी हाँ, यह रजिस्टी-पत्र है ।

Yes Sir, it is a registered letter.
यस् सर्, इट् इज़् अ रजिस्टर्ड लेटर् ।

9. Kyā āpko iśkī pahuñch rasīd chāhiye ? क्या आपको इसकी पहुँच रसीद चाहिए ?	Do you want an acknowledgement of this letter ? डू यू वांट् अॅन् अक्नॉले-ज़मेंट ऑफ दिस लेटर् ?
10. Jī hān̐, muze iśkī pahuñch-rasīd chāhiye. जी हाँ, मुझे इसकी पहुँच-रसीद चाहिए।	Yes Sir, I want an acknowledgement of it. यस् सर्, आय् वांट् अॅन् एकनॉलेजमेंट ऑफ इट् ।
11. I glaṇḍ kī chiṭṭhī ke lie kitnā ṭikeṭ legegā ? इंग्लैण्ड की चिट्ठी के लिए कितना टिकट लगेगा ?	What's the postage for a letter to England ? व्हाटर्स् द् पोस्टेज फॉ- अ लेटर् टु इंग्लैण्ड ?
12. Ek mani-Orḍar fārm dījiye. एक मनि-ऑर्डर फार्म दीजिये ।	(Please) give me a money order form. (प्लीज़्) गिव् मी अ माने ऑर्डर फार्म ।
13. Chiṭṭhī ḍāk men̐ ḍālne ka ākhrī samay kyā hai? चिट्ठी डाक में डालने का आखिरी समय कब है ?	What's the latest hour for posting letters ? व्हाट्र्स् द् लेटेस्ट् अवर फॉ-पोस्टिंग लेटर्स ?

14. Din men kitnī bār dilivarī hotī hai ?
दिन में कितनी बार डिलिवरी होती है ?

How many deliveries are in a day ?
हाउ मेनी डिलिवरीज़ आर्-इन् अ डे ?

15. Kyā sabhī chiṭṭhiyān ear-mel se jātī hain ?
क्या सभी चिट्ठियाँ एअरमेल से जाती हैं ?

Do all letters go by air-mail ?
डू आल लेटर्स गो बाय् एअर्-मेल् ?

16. Main ese ear mel se bhejnā chāhtā hūn.
मैं इसे एअर-मेल से भेजना चाहता हूँ।

I want to send this by air-mail.
आय् वांट टु सेंड् दिस् बाय् एअर-मेल।

17. Parsal rajistrī ke liye kitnī fīs denī paḍtī hai ?
पार्सल रजिस्ट्री के लिए कितनी फीस देनी पड़ती है ?

Whats the fee for registering a parcel ?
व्हाट्स् द् फी फॉर्- रेजिस्टरिंग् अ पार्सल् ?

18. Mere nām se koī dāk hai ?
Merā nām ....
मेरे नाम से कोई डाक है ?
मेरा नाम ....

Is there any mail for me ?
My name is...............
इज़् देअर्- एनी मेल् फॉर्- मी ?
माय् नेम् इज़् ....

19. Ghaŕ se chiṭṭhī ka intjāŕ hai.	I expect a letter from home .
घर से चिट्ठी का इन्तजार है ।	आय् एक्स्पेक्ट अ लेटर् फ्रॉम् होमॅ ।
20. Yaĥ merā parichaý-pat a hai.	Here's my identity card.
यह मेरा परिचय-पत्र है ।	हिअॅ-ज़् माय् आइडेन्टिटी कार्ड़ ।
21. Dāḱ abhī āyī hai. Dekhta hu	The mail has just received. Let me see.
डाक अभी आयी है । देखता हूँ।	द मेल हैज़ जस्ट् रिसीव्ह्ड् । लॅट मी सी।

Telephone Talk : टेलिफोन पर बातचीत

टेलिफोन	Teliphoń	Telephone	टेलिफोन
टेलिफोन-नंबर्	Teliphoń nambaŕ	Telephone number	टेलिफोन नंबर्
टेलिफोन कॉल	Teliphoń koľ	Telephone Call	टेलिफोन कॉल्
एक्सटेशन् कॉल	Exteńṣań koľ	Extension Call	एकस्टेशन् कॉल्
ह्लो	hălo	Hello	ह्लो
पर्सनल कॉल	Parsonaĺ koľ	Personal Call	पर्सनल् कॉल्

टेलिफोन	Teliphoń	Telephone	टेलिफोन
डाइरेक्टरी	ḍirektarī	directory	डिरेक्टरी
Receiver	रिसीवर्	Operator	ऑपरेटर्
Engaged	इंगेज़्ड	Cut off	कट् ऑफ्
nādurust	नादुरूस्त	Out of order	ऑउट ऑफ आर्डर्
galat nambaŕ	ग़लत नंबर	Wrong number	राँग् नंबर
Pratikriyā nahīn̐	प्रतिक्रिया नहीं		
No response	नो रिस्पॉन्स्	ṕratyuttaŕ nahīn̐	प्रत्युत्तर नहीं

1. Āṕkā (āṕke liye) phoń hai. There is a telephone call for you.

आपका (आपके लिये) फोन है । देअर्- इज़् अ टेलिफोन् कॉल फॉ- यू ।

2. Koyī pratikriyā nahīn̐ hai. There is no response.
कोई प्रतिक्रिया नहीं है । देअर्- इज़् नो रिस्पॉन्स् ।

3. Lā-i-n chālū hai. The line is engaged.
लाइन चालू है । द् लाइन् इज़् इंगेज़्ड् ।

4. Phoń kharab hai. The phone is out of order.
फोन खराब है । द् फोन इज़् ऑउट् ऑफ ऑर्डर ।

5. Kiś namberí se bāt́ kar rahe hain̐ ?
किस नंबर से बात कर रहे हैं ?

What number are you calling ?
व्हाट् नंबर आर्- यू कालिंग ?

6. Halo ! Main̐ .... bol rahā hūn̐.
हलो, ! मैं .... बोल रहा हूँ ।

Hello ! I .... am speaking.
हलो ! आय् .... आम् स्पीकिंग ।

7. Muze .... unse bāten̐ karanī hain̐, K ipaya, āp unhen̐ phoń par bulāye ge ?
मुझे .... उनसे बातें करनी हैं, कृपया आर्प उन्हें फोन पर बुलायेंगे ?

I want to speak to Mr. .... would you please call him on phone ?
आय् वाट् टु स्पीक् टु मिस्टर .... वुड् यू प्लीज़् कॉल् हिम् ऑन् फोन् ?

8. K ipýā phoń liye rahen̐.
कृपया, फोन लिये रहें ।

Hold the line, please.
होल्ड् द लाइन् , प्लीज़् ।

9. Halo ! iś samaý ve bāhaŕ gaye huye hain̐.
हलो ! इस समय वे बाहर

Hello ! He is out at the moment.
हलो ! ही इज़् ऑउट् अॅट् द

गये हुए हैं ।

मोमेंट् ।

10. Jab́ ve lauṭen, k ipýā uńse muze phoń karne ko kahen̐, Mera nāḿ ....

जब वे लौटें, कृपया उनसे मुझे फोन करने को कहें । मेरा नाम .... है ।

When he will be back, please tell him to call! me My name is ....

व्हेन् ही विल् बी बैक्, प्लीज़् टेल् हिम् टु कॉल् मी. माय् नेम् इज़्..................

1.Āṕ ek' baŕ fir kosiṣ karen̐.

आप एक बार फिर कोशिश करें ।

Would you please try again.

वुड् यू प्लीज ट्राय् अगेन् ।

At the Telegraph Office : तार-घर में

Tāŕ-ghaŕ kahān̐ hai ?

तार-घर कहाँ है ?

Where is the Telegraph Office ?

व्हेअर्- इज़् दॅ टेलिग्राफ् ऑफिस् ?

Muze tāŕ kaŕnā hai.

मुझे तार करना है ।

I've a telegram to send.

आय्र्व् अ टेलिग्राम् टु सेन्ड् ।

K ipýa telegraph fārm dījiye.

कृपया टेलिग्राफ-फॉर्म दीजिये ।

May I please have a form ?

मे आय् प्लीज़् हैव् अ फॉर्म् ?

Prati śabd kyā daŕ hai ?	How much is it per word ?
प्रति शब्द क्या दर है ?	हाउ मच् इज़् इट् पर वर्ड ?
Orḍinarī bhejnā chāhte hain̐ yā expres ?	Do you want to send it ordinary of express ?
आर्डिनरी भेजना चाहते हैं या एक्स्प्रेस ?	डू यू वांट् टु सेंड् इट् ऑर्डिनरी ऑ- एक्सप्रेस् ?
Expres, Sāhb !	Express, Sir.
एक्प्रेस, साहब !	एक्स्प्रेस्, सर् ।
Lanḍań kebal kaŕne ke liye kitnā samay lagegā ?	How long will a cable to London, take ?
लंडन केबल करने के लिए कितना समय लगेगा ?	हाउ लाँग विल् अ केबल् टु लंडन टेक् ?

तार	tār	telegram	टेलिग्राम
तार-ऑफिस्	tār-ŏfis	telegraph-office	टेलिग्राफ-ऑफिस्
तार का फार्म	taŕ-kā-farḿ	telegram form	टेलिग्राम - फॉर्म
एक्सप्रेस	expres	express	एक्स्प्रेस्
ऑर्डिनरी	Orḍinarī	ordinary	ऑर्डिनरी
प्रति शब्द	Prati-śabd	per-word	पर-वर्ड
समुद्री तार	Samudrī taŕ	cable	केबल्
समुद्र में	Samudra men̐	cable gram	केबल्ग्राम्

से भेजे जाने का तार	se bheje jāne kā tāŕ	

At the Restaurant : रेस्टरॉ में

1. Kisī restarān̐ men̐ chalen. किसी रेस्तराँ में चलें ।	Let us go to some restaurant. लेट् अस् गो टु सम रेस्टराँ.
2. Dekhiye, vahān̐ vaḿ tebaĺ khālī hai ? देखिये, वहाँ वह टेबल् खाली है ?	Excuse me, is that table over there is vacant ? एक्स्क्यूज़् मी, इज़् दैट् टेबल ओव्हर देअर्- वेकंट् ?
3. Jī, use āṕ le saḱte hain̐. जी, उसे आप ले सकते हैं।	Yes, Sir, you may take it. येस्, सर, यू मे टेक् इट् ।
4. Sāhaḃ ! āṕ kyā le ge ? साहब, आप क्या लेंगे ?	Sir, What would you like to take ? सर, व्हाट् वुड् यू लाइक टु टेक् ?
5. Minu dekhen̐ ? मीनू देखें ?	Where is the menu ? व्हेअर इज़् द मेनू ?
6. Hān̐, Sāhaḃ ! yaḿ menu hai. हाँ, साहब ! यह मेनू है।	Yes, Sir, here is the menu. येस सर् हिअर्- इज़् द मेनू ।

7. Hān̐, Sāhab ! kyā lenā chāhe ge ? हाँ, साहब ! क्या लेना चाहेंगे ?	Sir, What would you like to take ? सर, व्हाट् वुड् यू लाइक् टु टेक् ?
8. kăphi lā-o. कॉफी लाओ ।	Bring coffeé. ब्रिंग् कॉफी ।
9. Kaun-sī kăphī ? कौन-सी कॉफी ?	What type of coffee ? व्हाट् टाइप् ऑफ् कॉफी ?
10. Garam kăphī. गरम कॉफी ।	I want hot cottee . आय् वांट् हॉट् कॉफी ।
11. Kuchh khane ko le ge, Sāhab ? कुछ खाने को लेंगे, साहब ?	Will you take anything to eat ? विल् यू टेक् एनिथिंग् टु इट् ?
12. Suno, pahle do plet panīr pakauḍā lā-o' bād men̐ do plet vegitebal katlet. Ākhir men̐ do pyālī garam-garam kaphi lānā. सुनो, पहले दो प्लेट	Listen, first bring two plates of paneer pakauḍa and then two plates of vegitable cutlet. After that you may bring two cups of hot coffee. लिसन् , फर्स्ट् ब्रिंग् टू प्लेट्स्

पनीर पकौड़ा लाओ बाद में दो प्लेट् व्हेजिटेबल् कटलेट्। आखिर में दो प्याली गरम-गरम कॉफी लाना	ऑफ पनीर पकौड़ा ॲण्ड् देन् टू प्लेट्स् ऑफ् व्हेजिटेबल् कटलेट्। आफ्टर देट् यू मे ब्रिंग् टू कप्स् ऑफ् हॉट कॉफी ।
13. Kyā āp itnā hī chāhte hain, Sahab !	Is this all you want, Sir !
क्या आप इतना ही चाहते हैं साहब !	इज़् दिस् आल् यू वांट्, सर् !
14. Jarā jaldī le ā-o,	Bring it quickly, please.
जरा जल्दी ले आओ, ।	ब्रिंग् इट् क्विक्लि प्लीज़् ।
15. Jī, Sahab !	Yes, Sir.
जी, साहब !	येस्, सर् ।
16. Panīr Pakauḍā, sāhab !	Here is panir, Pakauḍa, Sir.
पनीर् पकौड़ा, साहब !	हिअर्- इज़् पनीर् पकौड़ा, सर ।
17. Jarā idhar namak sarkāye ge ?	Might I trouble you for salt ?
जरा इधर नमक सरकायेंगे ?	माइट् आय् ट्रबल् यू फॉ साल्ट् ?
18. Vegitabal katlet, sāhab !	Here is vegetable cutlet, Sir !
व्हेजिटेबल कटलेट्, साहब !	हिअर्- इज़् वेजिटेबल् कट्लेट्, सर् !

19. Auŕ kuchh́, Sahab́ ? और कुछ, साहब !	Anything more, Sir ? एनिथिंग् मोर्́ , सर् ?
20. Ab́ garaḿ-garaḿ kaphi lā-o. अब गरम-गरम कॉफी लाओ ।	Now, you bring hot coffee. नाउ, यू ब्रिंग हौट् कॉफी ।
21. Krīḿ ke sāth́ yā binā krīḿ kī ? क्रीम के साथ या बिना क्रीम की ?	With cream or without cream ? विद् क्रीम् ऑर विदाउट् क्रीम ?
22. Krīḿ ke sath क्रीम के साथ ।	With cream. विद् क्रीम् ।
23. Jaldī karo, bhā-ī. जल्दी करो, भाई ।	Be quick, please. बी क्विक्, प्लीज़् ।
24. Garaḿ-garaḿ kăphi, Sāhab́ ! गरम-गरम कॉफी, साहब ।	Here is hot coffee, Sir ! हिअर्- इज़् हॉट् कॉफी, सर ।
25. Daś minat́ ke bād bil̍ lānā.	Bring the bill after ten minutes.

दस मिनट के बाद बिल लाना। — ब्रिंग् द बिल् आफ्टर् टेन् मिनट्स् ।

26. Yah hai bil, Sāhab . — It is your bill, Sir.
यह है बिल, साहब । — इट् इज़् यॉ बिल्, सर् ।

27. Yah pachās kā noṭ le jā-o. — Take this fifty rupees note.
यह पचास का नोट ले जाओ । — टेक् दिस् फिफ्टि रुपीज़् नोट् ।

28. Bākī ke rupye, Sahab ! — Here is your remaining money, Sir.
बाकी के रुपये, साहब ! — हिअर्- इज़् यॉ रिमेनिंग् मनि, सर् ।

29. Yah rahī tumhari backhṣīṣ. — Here is the tip for you.
यह रही तुम्हा बख्शीश । — हिअर्- इज़् द टिप् फॉ यू ।

30. Dhanyavād Sāhab ! — Thank you, Sir.
धन्यवाद, साहब ! — थैंड्क यू, सर् ।

At tne Hotel : होटल में

1. Āgantuk - Namaste, Jī ! — Visitor—Goodmorning, Sir!
आगंतुक - नमस्ते, जी ! — विजिटर– गुड् मार्निंग्, सर् !

2. Svāgaṫ kartā — Namaste, Sāhab́ !

स्वागतकर्ता नमस्ते, साहब !

Receptionist–Good moring, Sir !

रिसेप्शनिस्ट्– गुड् मोर्निंग् , सर् !

3. Āgantuḱ— Kyā eḱ kaḿrā milegā ?

आगंतुक– क्या एक कमरा मिलेगा ?

Visitor— Can I have a room?

विजिटर्– कॅन् आय् हॅव्ह् अ रूम् ?

4. Svāgaṫ kartā— Avaśý ! Āṕkā śubh nāḿ ?

स्वागतकर्ता– अवश्य ! आपका शुभनाम ?

Receptionist— Certainly, May I know your good Please ?

रिसेप्सनिस्ट्– सर्टेन्लि, मे आय् नो यॉ- गुड् नेम्, प्लीज् ।

5. Āgantuḱ– Avināś Chataŕjī.

आगतुक–अविनाश चटर्जी ।

Visitor— Avinash́ Chatteŕji.

विजिटर्–अविनाश चटर्जी ।

6. Svāgaṫkartā— Āṕ kahān se āye hain̐ ?

Receptionist— From where have you come ?

स्वागतकर्ता– आप कहाँ से आये हैं ?

रिसेप्सनिस्ट्– फ्रॉम् व्हेअर हॅव्ह् यू कम ?

7. Āgantuk— Kalkattā se.

आगंतुक– कलकत्ता से ।

Visitor— From Calcutta.

विजिटर्– फ्रॉम् कॅलकटा ।

8. Svāgatkartā— Āpkā kyā vyav'sāy hai ?

स्वागतकर्ता– आपका क्या व्यवसाय है ?

Receptionist— What do you do ?

रिसेप्सनिस्ट्– व्हाट् डू यू डू ?

9. Āgantuk— Main Bangal kemikal kampnī kā pratinidhi hūn.

आगंतुक– मैं बंगाल केमिकल कम्पनी का प्रतिनिधि हूँ।

Visitor— I am representing Bengal Chemical Company

विजिटर्– आय् ॲम् रिप्रेसेंटिंग् बंगाल केमिकल कम्पनी ।

0. Svāgatkartā— Kitne din ṭhaharne kā vichār hai, Sāhab ?

स्वागतकर्ता– कितने दिन ठहरने का विचार है, साहब ?

Receptionist— How long do you plan to stay, Sir ?

रिसेप्सनिस्ट्– हाउ लॉंग डू यू प्लॅान् टु स्टे, सर् ?

11. Āgantuk— Ek Saptāh . Visitor— I may stay for a week.

आगंतुक– एक सप्ताह । विजिटर्– आय् मे स्टे फॉ अ वीक् ।

12. Svāgatkartā—kaisā kamrā pasand hai ? Receptionist— Which type of room you will like ?

स्वागतकर्ता–कैसा कमरा पसन्द है ? रिसेप्सनिस्ट्– व्हिच् टाइप् ऑफ रूम यू विल् लाइक् ?

13. Āgantuk— Bāg kī o-r barāmade vāla singal kamrā. Visitor—I would like a single room with balcony facing the garden.

आगंतुक– बाग की ऑर बरामदे वाला सिंगल कमरा । विजिटर्– आय् वुड् लाइक् अ सिंगल रूम विद् बालकनि फेसिंग् द गार्डन् ।

14. Svāgatkarta— Kis manjile par ? Receptionist– On which storey ?

स्वागतकर्ता– किस मंजिल पर ? रिसेप्स्निस्ट्– ऑन् व्हिच् स्टोरि ?

15. Āgantuk— Ach-chhā rahegā, agar pahlī manjil par mil jā-e Visitor— It will be better, if it is at the first floor.

आगंतुक– अच्छा रहेगा, अगर पहली मंजिल पर मिल जाए ।	विजिटर्– इट् विल् बी बेटर्, इफ् देअर्- इज़् ॲट् द फर्स्ट फ्लोर्।
16. Svāgatkartā— Jarā ruken, muze dekhne den.	Receptionist— Just wait a minute; let me see.
स्वागतकर्ता– जरा रुकें, मुझे देखने दें।	रिसेप्स्निस्ट्– जस्ट् वेट् अ मिनट, लेट् मी सी ।
17. Āgantuk— Main kamrā dekhūn ?	Visitor—May I see the room?
आगंतुक– मैं कमरा देखूँ ?	विजिटर्- मे आय् सी द रूम् ?
18. Āgantuk— Kyā is-se ach-chhā nahīn hai ?	Visitor— Have you nothing better ?
आगंतुक– क्या इससे अच्छा नहीं है ?	विजिटर्– हॅव्ह् यू नथिंग् बेटर् ?
19. Svāgatkartā— Sabhī uṭh gaye hain.	Receptionist— All are booked.
स्वागतकर्ता- सभी उठ गये हैं ।	रिसेप्स्निस्ट्– आल आ बुक्ड् ।
20. Āgantuk— Ach-chhā, yahī kamrā sahī.	Visitor— Well. I'll take this room.

आगंतुक– अच्छा, यही कमरा सही । | विजिटर्– वेल्. आई विल् टेक दिस् रूम् ।

21. Āgantuk— iś (kamre) kā kyā kirāya hai ?
आगंतुक– इस (कमरे) का क्या किराया है ?

Visitor— What is the charge for this room ?
विजिटर्– व्हाट् इज़् द चार्ज फॉ दिस् रूम् ?

22. Svāgatkartā— painsaṭh rupye pratī din, ek naste ke sāth aur subaḥ -ṣam do chāy

Receptionist— Rupees 65/- per day, with a breakfast and two-tea morning and evening.

स्वागतकर्ता– पैंसठ रुपये प्रतिदिन; एक नाश्ते के साथ ऑर सुबह-शाम दो चाय।

रिसेप्स्निस्ट्– रुपीज़् 65/- पर डे, विद् अ ब्रेकफास्ट् अैण्ड टू टी-मोर्निंग ऑण्ड् इव्हिनिंग् ।

23. Āgantuk— Kyā kuchh pesgī denī hai ?
आगंतुक– क्या कुछ पेशगी देनी है ?

Visitor— Have I to pay an advance ?
विजिटर्– हॅवआय् टु पे अन् ॲड्वांस् ?

24. Svāgatkartā— Oh, nahīn, Sāhab !

Receptionist— Oh, No, Sir.

स्वागतकर्ता– ओह, नहीं, साहब !

रिसेप्सनिस्ट्– ओह, नो, सर् ।

25. Āgantuk— Dhanyavād.

आगंतुक– धन्यवाद ।

Visitor— Thank you, So much.

विजिटर्– थैङ्क यू, सो मच् ।

26. Āgantuk— Kṛipyā merā sāmān ūpar āne den.

आगंतुक– कृपया मेरा सामान ऊपर आने दें ।

Visitor— Have my luggage taken up, please.

विजिटर्– हैव्ह् मॉय लगेज् टेकन् अप् प्लीज् ।

27. Āgantuk— Chābhī kahān rakh chhoḍūn ?

आगंतुक– (1) चाभी कहाँ रख छोड़ूँ ?

Visitor— (1) Where must I leave my key ?

विजिटर– व्हेअर मस्ट् आय् लीव् माय् की ?

28. Hotal kab band hotā hai ?

(2) हॉटेल कब बंद होता है ?

(2) When does the gates of hotel close?

व्हेन् डज़् द गेट्स ऑफ हॉटेल क्लोज़् ?

29. Kyā rāt bhar khulā rahtā hai ?

(3) क्या रात भर खुला रहता है ?

(3) Is it open whole night ?

इज़् इट् ओपन् व्होल् नाइट् ?

30. Āgantuk— (1) Kal main̐ jā rahā hūn̐.	Visitor— (1) I am leaving to-morrow.
आगंतुक– (1) कल मैं जा रहा हूँ।	विजिटर– आय् ॲम् लीविंग् टु-मॉरो।
31. — Kripyā bil banā den̐.	(2) Please have my bill made out.
(2) कृपया बिल बना दें ।	प्लीज़् हॅव् माय् बिल मेड् आउट् ।
32. — Kripyā āp is pate par mere patra bhijvā den̐.	(3) Will you have my letters sent on this address ?
(3) कृपया आप इस पते पर मेरे पत्र भिजवा दें ।	विल् यू हॅव् माय् लेटर्स सेंट् ऑन् दिस् अड्रेस् ?
33. (4) Sāmān nīche man̐gvā len̐.	Have the luggage brought down.
सामान नीचे मँगवा लें ।	हॅव् दॅ लगेज़् ब्रॉट् डाउन् ।
34. Dhanyavād.	Thank you.
धन्यवाद ।	थैंक् यू ।
35. Achchhā, jate hain̐, Namaste.	(6) Well we go Namaste.
अच्छा, जाते हैं, नमस्ते।	वेल् वी गो नमस्ते ।

36. Svāgatkarta— Namaste. Namaste.
स्वागतकर्ता– नमस्ते ।

Receptiionist— Good bye,
रिसेप्शनिस्ट्– गुड् बाय्,

At the Watch-maker's : घड़ीसाज की दुकान में

1. Ghaḍīsāj— Namaste, Sāhab !
घड़ीसाज़– नमस्ते, साहब !

Watchmaker—Good morning, Sir.
वाच्मेकर– गुड् मॉर्निंग्, सर् ।

2. Grāhak— Namaste .
ग्राहक– नमस्ते ।

Customer— Good morning.
कस्टमर्– गुड् मॉर्निंग् ।

3. Ghaḍīsāj— Kyā hukm hai ?
घड़ीसाज़– क्या हुक्म है ?

Watchmaker— What can I do for you sir.
वाच्मेकर्– व्हाट् कॅन् आय् डू फॉ यू सर् ?

4. Grāhak— Jarā meri ghaḍī dekhenँ yah hamesā pīchhe rahtī hai.
ग्राहक- जरा, मेरी घड़ी देखें, यह हमेशा पीछे रहती है ।

Customer— I want you to have a look at my watch. It's always slow.
कस्टमर- आय् वांट् यू टु ह्वॅ अ लुक् ॲट् माय् वाच्। इट्स् आलेवज् स्लो ।

5. Ghaḍīsaj— Dekhūn.
घड़ीसाज़– देखूँ ।

Watchmaker— Let me have a look at it.
वाच्मेकर्– लेट् मी ह्रॅव् अ लुक् ॲट् इट् ।

6. Ghaḍīsāj— mashīń ke ander bahut gandgī hai. Iśkī saphā-ī kańnī hogī.
घड़ीसाज़– क्यों नहीं ? मशीन के अंदर बहुत गंदगी है। इसकी सफाई करनी होगी ।

Watchmaker— There is a lot of dirt in it. It needs a cleaning.
वाच्मेकर्– देअ्र इज ए लॉट आफ डर्ट इन इट। इट नीड्स अं क्लीनिंग्।

7. Grāhak— Kitne diń lage ge ?
ग्राहक– कितने दिन लगेंगे ?

Customer— How long will it take ?
कस्टमर्– हाउ लॉग् विल् इट् टेक् ?

8. Ghaḍīsāj— Kań se kam do diń, Sāhab !
घड़ीसाज– कम से कम दो दिन, साहब !

Watchmaker— At least two days, Sir.
वाच्मेकर्– ॲट् लीस्ट् टू डेज़्, सर् ।

9. Grāhak— Kab taiyār ho jāyegā ?

Customer— When will it be ready ?

ग्राहक– कब तैयार हो जायेगा ?

कस्टॅमर्– व्हेन् विल् इट् बी रेडी ?

10. Ghaḍīsāj– Parsoṅ

Watchmaker— Day after to-morrow.

घड़ीसाज– परसों ।

वाच्मेकर्– डे आफ्टर् टु-मॉरो ।

11. Grāhak– Āj Somvār hai, kal Maṅgalvār hogā, aur parsoṅ Budhvār hogā ! Bahut ach-chhā, Maiṅ Guruvār kī shām ko Ghaḍī lene āūṅgā.

Customer— To-day is Monday, To-morrow will be Tuesday, and day after tomorrow will be Wednesday. Well, I shall come and collect it on Thursday evening.

ग्राहक– आज सोमवार है कल मंगलवार होगा, और परसों बुधवार होगा । बहुत अच्छा, मैं गुरुवार की शाम घड़ी लेने आऊँगा ।

कस्टॅमर– टु-डे-इज़् मंडे, टु-मॉरो विल् बी टयूस्डे, ॲण्ड् डे-आफ्टर्-टु-मॉरो विल् बी वेनैज्-डे। वेल् , आय् शल् कम् ॲण्ड् कैलेक्ट इट् ऑन् थर्ज़-डे इवनिंग् ।

12. Ghaḍīsāj– Bahut ach-chhā, Sāhab !

Watchmaker All right Sir, Good day, Sir.

Namaste.

घड़ीसाज़– बहुत अच्छा, साहब ! नमस्ते ।

वाच्मेकर्– आल राइट सर् गुड् डे, सर् ।

13. Grāhak— Namaste.

ग्राहक– नमस्ते ।

Customer— Good day.

कस्टमर्– गुड् डे ।

At the Cloth-shop : कपड़े की दुकान में

1. Grāhak— Ko-ī kuŕti kā kapḍā dikhāye ge ?

ग्राहक– कोई कुरति का कपड़ा दिखायेंगे ?

Customer— Will you show me cloth for doublet ?

कस्टमर्– विल यू शो मी क्लौथ फॉं डबलिट् ?

2. Vikretā— Avaśy, kaun-sā kapḍā dikhāūn̐, Mān̐, Jī ! Mān̐, ji.

विक्रेता– अवश्य, कौन-सा कपड़ा दिखाऊँ ? माँ जी ! माँ जी !

Salesman— Ofcourse, which cloth you would like to see,

सेल्समैन्– ऑफ कोर्स्, व्हिच् क्लॉथ यू वुड् लाइक् टु सी,

3. Grāhak— Ṭeriliṇ ya ṭerikoṭ

ग्राहक– टेरिलिन् या टेरिकॉट् ।

Customer— Terrylin or terrycot.

कस्टमर्– टेरिलिन् आॅ टेरिकॉट् ।

4. Kuchh auŕ namūne

Can you show me some

dikhāye ge ? कुछ ऑर नमूने दिखाएगे ?	more? कॅन् यू शो मी सम मोर´ ?
5. Muze yah ra ǵ pasa d nahīn̐. मुझे यह रंग पसंद नहीं।	I don't like this colour ´आय् डों´ट् लाइक´ दिस् क़लर् ।
6. Muze gā hhā ra ǵ nahīn̐ chāhiye. मुझे गाढ़ा रंग नहीं चाहिये ।	I don't need dark shade. आय् डों´ट् नीड् डार्क् शेड्´ ।
6. Halkā ra ǵ dikha-i-ye. हल्का रंग दिखाइये ।	Show me light shade. शो मी लाइट् शेड् ।
8. Muze 'sho-keś' vālā pasa d́ hai. मुझे शो–केस´वाला पसंद है ।	I like the one in the show-case. आय् लाइक्´ द´ वन्´ इन द´ शो–केस्´।
9.Hān̐, magaŕ muze phīkā ra ǵ chāhiye. हाँ, मगर मुझे फीका रंग चाहिये ।	Yes, but I want a light colour. येस्, बट् आय् वांट् अ लाइट् कलर् ।
10. Hān̐, vah hai jiśkī talāṣ men̐	That's what I was looking

main̐ the. | for.
हाँ वह है जिसकी तलाश में मैं थी। | दैट्र्स् व्हाट् आय् वाज़् लुकिंग् फॉर्

11. Kaise mīṭaŕ diyā ? | How much is that per metre ?
कैसे मीटर दिया ? | हाउ मच् इज़् दैट् पर् मीटर् ?

12. Vikretā— .... Rupýe mītaŕ mān̐ jī. | Salesman— .... rupees per metre, Mān̐ jī.
विक्रेता– .... रुपय मीटर, माँ जी । | सेल्स्मॅन्– .... रुपीज् पर मीटर, माँ जी ।

13. Grāhak— Tīń mītaŕ phāḍ den̐. | Customer— Make it three metres.
ग्राहक– तीन मीटर फाड़ दें। | कस्टमर्– मेक् इट् थ्री मीटर्स ।

14. Vikretā— Iśke sāth dupttā le ge ? | Salesman— Would you like to have Dupatta with it ?
विक्रेता– इसके साथ दुपट्टा लेंगें ? | सेल्स्मॅन्– वुड् यू लाइक् टु हॅव दुपट्टा विद् इट् ?

15. Grāhak— Jarūŕ Iś kuŕte ke | Customer—Certainly, I want

anu'rūp hī vah chāhīye. | something to match this.
ग्राहक– जरूर, इस कुरते के अनुरूप ही वह चाहिये । | कस्टमर्– सर्टेन्लि, आय् वांट् सम ́थिंग् टु मॅच् दिस् ।

16. Vikretā— aur kuchh ? | Salesman— Anything else ?
विक्रेता– और कुछ ? | सेल्स्मॅन्– एनिथिंग् एल्स् ?

17. Grāhak— Na, abhī kuchh nahīn. | Customer— No, Nothing, at present.
ग्राहक– न, अभी कुछ नहीं | कस्टमर्– नो, नथिंग्, ॲट् प्रेजंट् ।

18. Kripyā bil den | Please, give me the bill.
कृपया बिल दें । | प्लीज़् , गिव् मी द ́ बिल् ।

19. Ye āpke paise. | Please take it.
ये आपके पैसे । | प्लीज टेक इट ।

20. Vikretā— Dhanyavād, Mānjī ! Namaste.! | Salesman—Thank you, Mān jī ! Namaste.
विक्रेता– धन्यवाद, माँ जी ! नमस्ते ! | सेल्स्मॅन्– थॅड्क् यू, माँ जी ! नमस्ते

At the Green-Grocer's : शाक–सब्जी की दुकान में

1. Māph́ kījiye, Sāhab́, s̒āk-sabjī kahān̐ milen̐gī ?	Excuse me, Sir, where I can find vegetables ?
माफ कीजिये, साहब, शाक सब्जी कहाँ मिलेंगी ?	एक्स्क्यूज़् मी सर् , व्हेअर् आय् कॅन् फाइंड् वेजिटेबल्स् ?
2. Yahān̐ se laghbhaǵ eḱ pharlānǵ paŕ .	About a furlong from here.
यहाँ से लगभग एक फर्लांग पर ।	अबॉउट् अ फर्लांग् फ्रॉम् हिअर्- ।
3. Kahān̐ ?	Where ?
कहाँ ?	व्हेअर्- ?
4. Aglā nukkaḍ pāŕ kaŕ bāyīn̐ o-ŕ muḍiye.	Go to the next corner and turn left.
अगला नुक्कड़ पार कर बायीं ओर मुड़िये ।	गो टु दॅ नेक्सट् कॉर्नर् अॅण्ड् टर्न लेफ्ट् ।
5. Dhanyavād.	Thank you.
धन्यवाद ।	थॅङ्क् यू ।
6. Is̒men̐ kaisā ābhāŕ ?	No mention, please.
इसमें कैसा आभार ?	नो मेन्शन् , प्लीज़् ।
7. Tamātaŕ kaise diye ?	What is the price of tomato, please ?

टमाटर कैसे दिये ?	व्हाट् इज़् द प्राइस्' ऑफ् टॅमोटो, प्लीज़् ?
8. Chāŕ rupýe kilo, S̱āhab́ !	Four rupees a kilo, Sir.
चार रुपये किलो, साहब !	फोर् रुपीज़् अ किलो, सर् ।
9. Dō kilo do.	Give me two kilos.
दो किलो दो ।	गिव् मी टू किलोज़् ।
10. Bai gań tāje hain̈ ?	Have you fresh brinjals ?
बैंगन ताजे हैं ?	हॅव् यू फ्रेश़् ब्रिंजाल्स् ?
11. Hān̈, jī !	Yes, Sir !
हाँ, जी !	येस् , सर् !
12. Tāje nīle chhote gol bai gań idhaŕ hain̈.	Here are some fresh blue small round brinjals.
ताजे, नीले छोटे गोल बैंगन इधर हैं ।	हिअ्- आ सम् फ्रेश् ब्लू स्माल् राउंड् ब्रिंजाल्स् ।
13. Ek' kilo dō.	Give me one kilo.
एक किलो दो ।	गिव् मी वन् किलो ।
14. Bhāv' kyā ?	How do you sell them ?
भाव क्या ?	हाउ डू यू सेल् देम् ?
15. Dō rupýe pachāś paise,	Two rupees fifty paise

Sāhab́. — per kilo, Sir.

दो रुपये पचास पैसे, साहब । — टू रुपीज़् फिफ्टि पैसे पर् किलो, सर् ।

16. Dō rupýe men̐ doge kyā ? — Can you make it two rupees a kilo ?

दो रुपये में दोगे क्या ? — कॅन् यू मेक्ॅ इट् टू रुपीज़् अ किलो ?

17. Ná, paḍta nahīn̐ paḍtā, Sāhab́. — Sorry, I cannot offer it, Sir.

न, पड़ता नहीं पड़ता, साहब । — सॉरि, आय् कननाट् ऑफर इट्, सर् ।

18. Dekhiye sāhab́, ye mote man̐sal sahjan. — See Sir, these thick fleshy drum-sticks.

देखिये साहब, ये मोटे माँसल सहजन । — सी सर्, दीज़् थिक् फ्लेशि ड्रम्-स्टिक्स् ।

19. Kaise diye ? — How much is this ?

कैसे दिये ? — हाउ मच् इज़् दिस् ?

20. Rupýe ke chār sahjań. — Four sticks for a rupee.

रुपये के चार सहजन । — फोर्ॅ स्टिक्स् फॉ अ रुपी ।

21. Yá bahut maha gā hai.	It's rather costly.
यॅ बहुत महँगा है ।	इट्'स् रादर् कॉस्टलि ।
22. Yá bemausam kī chīj hai, Sāhab.	It's out of season, Sir.
यॅ बेमौसम की चीज है, साहब।	इट्स् आउट् ऑफ् सीजन् , सर् ।
23. Ach-chhā chalo, chār ye bhī de dō.	All right. Give four sticks of this too.
अच्छा चलो, चार ये भी दे दो ।	ऑल् राइट् गिव् फोर् स्टिक्स् ऑफ् दिस् टू।
24. Ye hain hare taje palak aur pudina.	These are green fresh spinach and mint.
ये हैं हरे ताजे पालक ऑर पुदीना ।	दीज़् आॅ ग्रीन फ्रेश् स्पिनाच् ॲण्ड् मिंट् ।
25. Kaise dīye ?	How do you sell them ?
कैसे दिये ?	हाउ डू यू सेल् देम् ?
26. Pālak pachās paise kī ek gaḍ-ḍī aur pudīnā rupye men.	Spinach fifty paise a pack and mint for a rupee.

पालक पचास पैसे की एक गड्डी ऑर पुदीना रुपये में ।	स्पिनाच् फिफ्टि पैसे अ पॅक् ॲण्ड् मिंट् फॉ अ रुपी ।
27. Inkī bhī ek-ek gad-dī rakh dō.	Keep a pack of each.
इनकी भी एक–एक गड्डी रख दो ।	कीप् अ पॅक् ऑफ् ईच् ।
28. Aur dekho, 50 gram adrak aur sau-sau grams hari mirch aur lahsun dō.	And also give me 50 gm ginger, 100 grammes each of chillis and garlics.
और देखो, 50 ग्रॉम् अदरक, और सौ–सौ ग्रॉम्स् हरी मिर्च ऑर लहसुन भी दो ।	ॲण्ड् आल्सो गिव् मी 50 ग्राम्स् जिंजर, 100 ग्राम्स ईच् ऑफ् लीज़् ॲण्ड् गारलिक्स ।
29. Māph kījiyegā, Sāhab, Abhi-abhī jo māl kheton se āyā hai, use āpne dekhā hī nahīn— Bhiṇḍī, Karelā, taro-ī, Sem, matar kī chhīmī, chichīṇdā, kelā, gājar, mūlī, pyāj, kaka hī,	Excuse me, Sir, you did not see the articles just arrived from the fields—lady's finger, bitter-gourd, angular gourd, beans, pease-cod, snake gourd, plantain. Carrot radish, onion, cucum-

kad-dū, konhḍā, ālū.	ber, bottle gourd, pumpkin, potato.
माफ कीजियेगा, साहब, अभी-अभी जो माल खेतों से आया है, उसे आपने देखा ही नहीं-भिंडी, करेला, तरोई, सेम, मटर की छीमी, चिचींडा, केला, गाजर, मूली प्याज, ककड़ी, कद्दू, कोंहड़ा, आलू ।	एक्सक्यूज़् मी, सर्, यू डिड् नॉट् सी द आर्टिकल्स् जस्ट् अराइवड् फ्रॉम् द फील्ड्स् लेडि ज़्, फिंगर्, बिटर् गोर्ड्, अँगुलर् गोर्ड्, बीन्स्, पीज़्-कॉड, स्नेक् गोर्ड्, प्लॅन्टेन्, कैरट रॅडिश, ऑनिअन्, कुकुम्बर, बॉटल् गोर्ड्, पम्पकिन्, पोटॅटो।
30. Dhanyavād, āj itnā hī. धन्यवाद, आज इतना ही ।	Thank you, That's all to-day. थॅड्क् यू, दॅट्'स् ऑल टु-डे ।
31. Muze kitnā denā hai ? मुझे कितना देना है ?	How much I owe you ? हाउ मच् आय् ओं यू ?
32. Adrak, mirch, auṙ lasuṅ ke 3.50 milākaṙ kul rupye 16.50 paise hote hain. अदरक, मिर्च ऑर लहसुन के 3.50 मिलाकर कुल रुपये 16.50	Including Rs. 3.50 paise of ginger, chilli and garlic, the total amount comes to Rs. 16.50 paise. इन्क्लुडिंग् रु० 3.50 पैसे ऑफ् जिंजर, चिलि ॲण्ड् गारलिक्, द टोटल अमॉउंट कम्स् टू रु.

पैसे होते हैं ।	16.50 पैसे

33. Yah lo.	Please have it.
यह लो ।	प्लीज हैव इट
34. Dhanyavād, Sāhab.	Thank you, Sir.
धन्यवाद, साहब ।	थैंड्क् यू, सर् ।

Seasons : मौसम (ऋतु)

1. Purvaiyā bah rahī hai.	The wind is flowing from the East.
पुरवैया बह रही है ।	दॅ विंड् इज़् फ्लाइंग् फ्रॉम् दॅ ईस्ट् ।
2. Yah Vasant hai.	It is the Spring
यह वसंत है ।	इट् इज़् दॅ स्प्रिंग् ।
3. Mastī lāyā hai.	It has brought the lust.
मस्ती लाया है ।	इट् हॅज़् ब्रॉट् दॅ लस्ट् ।
4. Duniyā pāgal ban gayī hai.	The world has become mad.
दुनिया पागल बन गयी है ।	दॅ वर्ल्ड् हैज़ बिकम् मैड् ।
5. Mausam suhāvanā hai.	The season is rejoicing one.

मौसम सुहावना है ।

द सीज़न् इज़् रिजॉयसिंग् वन् ।

6. Āj bahut garaḿ hai.

आज बहुत गरम है ।

It is very hot to-day.

इट् इज़् व्हेरि हॉट् टु-डे ।

7. Kyā manhūś diń hai !

क्या मनहूस दिन है !

What a wretched day !

व्हाट् अ रेचेड् डे !

8. Bilkul havā nahiń hai.

बिलकुल हवा नहीं है ।

Not a sign of wind.

नॉट् अ साइन ऑफ् विंड् ।

9. Āj bahut umaś hai.

आज बहुत उमस है ।

To-day is much sultriness.

टु-डे इज़् मच् सल्ट्रिनेस् ।

10. Pasīnā bah rahā hai.

पसीना बह रहा है ।

Sweat perspires.

स्वेट् परस्पायर्स् ।

11. Yah Grīṣḿ hai.

यह ग्रीष्म है ।

It is the Summer.

इट् इज़ द समर् ।

12. Āsmāń meń bādal chhāye haiń.

आसमान में बादल
छाये हैं ।

The sky is over-cast.

द स्काइ इज़ ओवर्-कॉस्ट् ।

13. An̐dherā hai. अँधेरा है ।	It is dark. इट् इज़ डार्क् ।
14. Varṣā hogī. वर्षा होगी ।	It will rain. इट् विल् रेन् ।
15. Bādal garajtā hai. बादल गरजता है ।	It thunders. इट् थंडर्स् ।
16. Bijlī chamaktī hai. बिजली चमकती है ।	It lightens. इट् लाइटन्स् ।
17. Varṣā jor se ho rahī hai. वर्षा जारे से हो रही है ।	It is pouring. इट् इज़् पोरिंग् ।
18. Mūsalādhār varṣā ho rahī hai. मूसलाधार वर्षा हो रही है ।	It is raining cats and dogs. इट् इज़् रेनिंग् कॅट्स् ॲण्ड् डॉग्स् ।
19. Pānī barasnā band hu-ā hai. पानी बरसना बंद	It has stopped raining. इट् हॅज़् स्टॉप्ड् रेनिंग् ।

हुआ है ।

20. Thaṇṭhī havā bah rahī hai. — A cool breeze is blowing.

ठंडी हवा बह रही है । — अ कूल ब्रीझ् इज़् ब्लोइंग् ।

21. Kyā tumhen yah mausam pasand hai ? — Do you like this weather ?

क्या तुम्हें यह मौसम पसंद है ? — डू यू लाइक् दिस् वेदर् ?

22. Varṣā sabhī ko suhātī hai. — Everyone likes the rainy season.

वर्षा सभी को सुहाती है । — एव्रि वन् लाइक्स् द रेनि सीज़न् ।

23. Isīliye sāvan men log peḍon se bandhe jhūlon men jhūlte hain. — Therefore people oscillate in swings tied with trees in Sāvan.

इसीलिए सावन में लोग पेड़ों से बधे झूलों में झूलते हैं । — देअर्-फोर' पीपल् ऑसिलेट् इन् स्विंग्स् टाइड् विद् ट्रीज़् इन सावन ।

24. Yah Suhāvanā mausam hai. — This is fine weather.

यह सुहावना मौसम
है ।

दिस् इज़् फाइन्´ वेदर् ।

25. Āśmāń sāph́ hai.
आसमान साफ है ।

The sky is clear.
द´स्काय् इज़् क्लीअर्´ ।

26. Peḍon̐ se chhańkaŕ
ṭhaṇḍhī havā bah́
rahī hai.
पेड़ों से छनकर
ठंडी हवा बह
रही है ।

Duly sieved by trees cool
breeze is blowing.
डयूलि सीव्व्ड् बाय् ट्रीज़् कूल्
ब्रीझ्´ इज़् ब्लोइंग् ।

27. Chān̐d́nī dudhiyā gayī hai.
चाँदनी दुधिया गयी है ।

The moonlight became milky.
द´मून् लाइट् बिकेम्´ मिल्कि ।

28. Yah́ śarad itu hai.
यह शरद् ऋतु है ।

It is Autumn.
इट् इज़् आटम् ।

29. Rāt men̐ ākāṣ tāron̐ se
jaǵmagātā hai.
रात में आकाश तारों से
जगमगाता है ।

During the night, the sky is
full of twinkling stars.
डयूरिंग् द´नाइट्, द´स्काय् इज़्
फुल् ऑफ् ट्विंक्लिंग् स्टार्स ।

30. Chān̐d́ dhaŕtī ko ṣabnaḿ
se nah́lātā hai.

The moon is giving bath to
the Earth with dews.

चाँद धरती को शबनम
से नहलाता है ।

द मून् इज़् गिविंग् बाथ् टु
द अर्थ् विद् ड्यूज़् ।

31. Āj bahut sardī hai.
आज बहुत सरदी है ।

It is very cold day.
इट् इज़् वेरि कोल्ड् डे ।

32. Yah Hemant hai.
यह हेमंत है ।

It is the cold season.
इट् इज़् द कोल्ड् सीज़न् ।

33. Sūraj din men̐ chamaktā hai.
सूरज दिन में चमकता है ।

The Sun shines during the day.
द सन् शाइन्स् ड्यूरिंग् द डे ।

34. Tarah-tarah kī havā-en̐ bah rahī hain̐.
तरह-तरह की हवाएँ बह रही हैं ।

Different kinds of wind blow.
डिफेरेंट् काइंड्स् ऑफ् विंड् ब्लो ।

35. Havā bahut chal rahī hai.
हवा बहुत चल रही है ।

It is windy.
इट् इज़् विंडि ।

36. Peḍon̐ se patte girte hain̐.
पेड़ों से पत्ते गिरते हैं ।

Leaves fall from trees.
लीव्ज़् फॉल् फ्रॉम् ट्रीज़् ।

37. Kheton̐ men̐ anāj pakte hain̐.

Grains ripe in the fields.

खेतों में अनाज पकते हैं ।	ग्रेन्स् राइप्ʼ इन् दʼ फील्ड्स् ।
38. Āj diń khulā hai.	To-day it is fine weather.
आज दिन खुला है ।	टु-डे इट् इज़् फाइन्ʼ वेदर् ।
39. Yaĥ s'is'ir hai.	It is s'is'ir .
यह शिशिर है ।	इट् इज़् शिशिर ।
40. Yaĥ suhāvanā mausam hai.	It is fine season.
यह सुहावना मौसम है।	इट् इज़् फाइन्ʼसीज़न ।

5 CLASSIFIED VOCABULARIES : वर्गीकृत शब्दावली

Colour	:	रंग
Flowers and leaves	:	फूल और पत्ते
Trees and their parts	:	वृक्ष और उसके अवयव
Dry-Fruits and fruits	:	मेवे और फल
Vegetables and Greens	:	शाक-सब्जियाँ
Spices	:	मसाले
Birds	:	पक्षी
Beasts	:	पशु
Reptiles, worms and Insects	:	सरीसृप और कीड़े-मकोड़े
Parts of the Body	:	शरीर के अंग
Clothes and wearing appasels etc.	:	कपड़ेऔर पहनने के पोशाक
Ornaments	:	आभूषण
Jewels	:	रत्न
Relatives	:	सगे-संबंधी
Condition of the Body and Ailments	:	शारीरिक अवस्था और रोग
Musical Instruments	:	वाद्य
Minerals and metals	:	खनिज और धातु
Trades and professions	:	व्यापार और व्यवसाय
Domestic Articles	:	घरेलू सामान

AT A GLANCE

Colour : रंग

lāl	लाल	Red	रेड्
harā	हरा	Green	ग्रीन्
nīlā	नीला	Blue	ब्लू
pīlā	पीला	Yellow	येलो
saphed	सफेद	White	व्हाइट्
kālā	काला	Black	बलॅक्
jāmunī	जामुनी	Purple	परपल्
kesri	केसरी	Saffron	सॅफ्रॉन्
bai g nī	बैंगनी	Violet	वायोलेट्
gulābī	गुलाबी	Pink	पिंक्
rākhī	राखी	Ash colour	अॅश् कलर
sletī	स्लेटी	Blue gray	ब्ल्यू ग्रे
matmailā	मटमैला	Grey (dusty)	ग्रे (डस्टी)
bhūrā	भूरा	Brown	ब्राउन्
rūpharā	रूपहरा	Silver	सिल्वर्
Sindūrī	सिंदूरी	Scarlet	स्कारलेट्
nāra gī	नारंगी	Orange	ऑरेंज्
sun herā	सुनहरा	Golden	गोल्डन
pīlā bhūrā	पीला-भूरा	Beige	बीझ़
rang	रंग	Colour	कलर्

Flowers and Leaves. : फूल और पत्ते

peḍ	पेड़	Tree	ट्री
paudhā	पौधा	Plant	प्लाण्ट्
latā	लता	Creaper	क्रीपर्
ṭahnī	टहनी	Stem	स्टेम्
pattā	पत्ता	Leaf	लीफ्
kalī	कली	Bud	बड्
phūl	फूल	Flower	फ्लॉवर्
kāñṭā	काँटा	Thorn	थॉन्
ark kā pattā	अर्क का पत्ता	Leaf of Swallow wort	लीफ् ऑफ् स्वालो वर्ट
kele kā pattā	केले का पत्ता	Leaf of Plantain	लीफ् ऑफ् प्लॅन्टेन्
tulasī-dal	तुलसी-दल	Leaf of holy Basil	लीफ् ऑफ् होलि बेसिल्
dūrvā	दूर्वा	Agrostis Lincaris	अग्रोस्टिस् लिंकारिस्
pān kā pattā	पान का पत्ता	Betal leaf	बेटल् लीफ्
bel kā pattā	बेल का पत्ता	Leaf of Wood-apple	लीफ् ऑफ् वूड-ॲप्पल्
menhdī	मेंहँदी	Myrtle	मिर्टल्
ark	अर्क	Swallow wort	स्वालो वर्ट्

kaneŕ	कनेर	Oleander	ओलींडर
kamaĺ	कमल	Lotus	लोटस्
Kamalinī	कमलिनी	Lily	लिलि
keťkī	केतकी	Pandanus	पेंडानस्
kesaŕ	केसर	Saffron	सॅफ्रॉन्
guĺdā-udī	गुलदाउदी	Chrysanthemum	क्रिसॅन्थेमम्
guĺbanaf́ś́ā	गुलबनफशा	Violet	वायेलेट्
guĺbahāŕ	गुलबहार	Daiśy	डेज़ी
guĺmenh́dī	गुलमेंहदी	Balsam	बालसम्
gulab́	गुलाब	Rose	रोज़्
gendā	गेंदा	Marygold	मेरिगोल्ड
chamelī	चमेली	Jasmine	जॅस्मिन्
champā	चम्पा	Magnolia	मॅग्नोलिया
japā	जपा	China-rose	चाइना रोज़्
jūhī	जूही	Juhi, a kind of jasmine	जूही, अ काइंड ऑफ् जॅस्मिन
dhatūrā	धतूरा	Stramonium	स्ट्रामोनिअम्
naŕgiś	नरगिस	Narcissus	नरसिसस्
nīĺ	नील	Indigo	इंडिगो
palāś	पलाश	Butea	बूटी
bakuĺ	बकुल	Minusops elengi	मिनुसॉप्स् एलेंगि
babūĺ	बबूल	Acasia	अकासिआ
belā	बेला	a kind of	अ काइंड् ऑफ्

jasmine	जॅस्मिन		
belī	बेली	a kind of jasmine	अ काइंड् ऑफ् जॅस्मिन
moǵrā	मेागरा	a kind of jasmine	अ काइंड् ऑफ् जॅस्मिन
rajanī-gandhā	रजनी-गन्धा	Night-queen	नाइट्-क्वीन्
śiriṣ́	शिरीष		
sūryā-mukhī	सूर्यमुखी	Sunflower	सन् फ्लॉवर्
siŕpenchā	सिरपेंचा	Ivy	आयवि
semaĺ	सेमल	Silk-cotton	सिल्क-कॉटन्

Trees and their parts : वृक्ष और उसके अवयव

a kuŕ	अंकुर	Germ	जर्म्
amarūd́	अमरूद	Guava	ग्वावा
āḿ	आम	Mango	मॅङगो
imlī	इमली	Tamarind	टमरिंड्
kalaḿ	कलम	Craft	क्राफ्ट्
kalī	कली	Bud	बड्
kāṭh́	काठ	Wood	वूड्
kāṅṭā	काँटा	Thorn	थॉर्न्
guṭhĺī	गुठली	Stone	स्टोन
gond́	गोंद	Gum	गम्
chīḍ	चीड़	Pine	पाइन

chhāĺ	छाल	Bark	बार्क
chhiĺkā	छिलका	Skin, Rind	स्किन्, रिंड्
jaṭā	जटा (नारियल का)	Coir	कॉयर्
jaḍ	जड़	Root	रूट्
jīrā	जीरा	Stamen	स्टॅमेन्
Jhā-ū	झाऊ	Conifer	कोनिफर्
taȟnī	टहनी	Stem	स्टेम्
ḍāĺ	डाल	Branch	ब्रांच्
dhaḍ	धड़	Trunk	ट्रंक्
naś	नस	Fibre	फायबर्
pattī	पत्ती	Leaf	लीफ्
phūĺ	फूल	Flower	फ्लॉवर्
baŕgaď	बरगद	Banyan	बनिअन
babūĺ	बबूल	Acacia	अकासिआ
bīj́	बीज	Seed	सीड्
bāns̈ś	बाँस	Bamboo	बॉम्बू
bhoj́pat a	भोजपत्र	Birch	बर्च
mahogani	महोगनी	Mahogany	महोगनि
raś	रस	Juice	जूस
raśa	रेशा	Pulp	पल्प
śākhā	शाखा	Branch	ब्रांच्
saro	सरो	Cypress	सायप्रेस्
sāǵvān	सागवान	Teak	टीक्
sen̈hush	सेंहुड़	Cactus	कॅक्टस्

Dry-fruits and fruits : मेवे और फल

mevā	मेवा	Dry-fruit	ड्राय्-फ्रूट्
an̐jīr	अँजीर	Fig	फिग्
akhrot	अखरोट	Walnat	वाल्नट्
ālū bukhārā	आलू बुखारा	Peach	पीच्
kājū	काजू	Cashewnut	कॅश्यूनट्
kiś-miś	किशमिश	Raisin	रेज़िन्
khajūr	खजूर	Date	डेट्
chiraun̐jī	चिरौंजी	Chironji safida	चिरोंजी सफीडा
chilgojā	चिलगोजा	Pine-fruit	पाइन-फ्रूट्
jardālū	जर्दालू	Apricot	अप्रिकॉट्
pista	पिस्ता	Pista chio	पिस्ताचिओ
bādām	बादाम	Almond	आलमंड
munakkā	मुनक्का	Currant	करंट्
mūn̐gphalī	मूँगफली	Groundnut	ग्राउंड्नट्
nāriyal	नारियल	Coconut	कोकोनट्
phal	फल	Fruit	फ्रूट्
an̐gūr	अँगूर	Grapes	ग्रेप्स्
anannāś	अनन्नास	Pine-apple	पाइन् ॲप्पल्
anār	अनार	Pomegranate	पोमेग्रेनेट्
amrūd	अमरूद	Guava	ग्वावा

ān̐vaḍā	आँवड़ा	Emblic myrobalam	एम्ब्लिक मिरोबलन
āḍū	आडू	Peach	पीच्
āṁ	आम	Mango	मॅङ्गो
īkh́	ईख	Sugar-cane	सुगर-केन
imlī	इमली	Tamarind	टॅमरिंग्
kakḍī	ककड़ी	Cucumber	कुकुम्बर
kaṭhaĺ	कटहल	Jack-fruit	जॅक्-फ्रूट
kelā	केला	Banana	बनाना
nāriyaĺ	नारियल	Cocoanut	कोकोनट्
gājaŕ	गाजर	Carrot	कॅरट्
khaŕbūj́	खरबूज	Musk-melon	मस्क-मेलन्
taŕbūj́	तरबूज	Water-melon	वाटर्-मेलॉन्
naśpatī	नाशपती	Pear	पेर्अ
nīn̐bū	नींबू	Lemon (acid)	लेमन् (एसिड्)
jāmuṅ	जामुन	Black-berry	ब्लॅक्-बेरि
papītā	पपीता	Papaya	पपया
beĺ	बेल	Wood-apple	वुड्-ॲप्पल्
beŕ	बेर	Plum	प्लम्
makoý	मकोय	Straw-berry	स्ट्रा-बेरि
mosambī	मोसम्बी	Lemon (sweet)	लेमन् (स्वीट्)
rājberī	राज़बेरि	Raspberry	राज़बेरि

līchī	लीची	leechee	लीची
śakaŕkandi	शकरकंदी	Sweet-potato	स्वीट-पोटेटो
śarīphā	शरीफा	Custard-apple	कस्टर्ड-ॲप्पल्
śahtuť	शहतूत	Mulberry	मल-बरि
sa tarā	संतरा	Orange	ऑरेंज
sapoṭā	सपोटा	Sapota	सपोटा
seb́	सेब	Apple	ॲप्पल्
baḍhal	बड़्हल	Artocarpus lauch	आर्टोकार्पस् लाक्
rāmphal	रामफल	Custard-apple	कस्टर्ड-ॲप्पल
phālsā	फालसा	Grewie asiatica	ग्रेवी असिआटिका
karaundā	करौंदा	The gooseberry	दॅ गूज़बेरि
kamrakh́	कमरख	Auerrhoa Carambola	आरहो करमबोला

Vegetables and Greens : शाक-सब्जियाँ

śāk-sabjī	शाक-सब्जी	Vegetables	वेजिटेवलस्
taro-ī	तरोई	Angular-gourd	ॲंगुलर-गोर्ड
aru-ī	अरुई	Arum	अरम्
seḿ	सेम	Beans (green)	बीन्स् (ग्रीन)
pharāsbīń	फरासबीन	Beans (french)	बीन्स् (फ्रेंच्)
lobiyā	लोबिया	Beans (string)	बीन्स् (स्ट्रिंग्)

chukandaŕ	चुकंदर	Beat-root	बीट्-रूट
karelā	करेला	Bitter-gourd	बिटर-गोर्ड
baiǹgań	बैंगन	Brinjal	ब्रिंजाल्
bańd gobhī	बंदगोभी	Cabbage	कॅबेज्
gājaŕ	गाजर	Carrot	कॅरट्
phūĺ-gobhī	फूलगोभी	Cauliflower	कॉलिफ्लॉवर्
chakotarā	चकोतरा	Citron	सिट्रन्
lāĺ mirch́	लालमिर्च	Chilli	चिल्लि
nāriyaĺ	नारियल	Coconut	कोकोनट
dhaniyāǹ	धनियाँ (हरा)	Coriander (green)	कॉरिअण्डर् (ग्रीन)
kakaḍī	ककड़ी	Cucumber	कुकुम्बर्
sah́jań	सहजन	Drum-stick	ड्रम्-स्टिक्
sūrań	सूरन,	Elephant yam	एलिफॅण्ट यॅम्
jamīkańd	जमीकंद		
lah́suń	लहसुन	Garlic	गारलिक्
ad́araḱ	अदरक	Ginger	जिंजर्
khīrā	खीरा	Gourd	गोर्ड
sāǵ	साग	Greens	ग्रीन्स्
mū ǵphalī	मूँगफली	Groundnut	ग्राउंड्नट्
patu-ā	पटुआ	Hemp	हेम्प्
kaṭahaĺ	कटहल	Jack-fruit	जैक्-फ्रूट्

garī, bīj	गरी, बीज	Kernel	करनेल्
bhindī,	भिंडी,	Lady's, finger,	लेडिज् फिंगर्,
rāmtaro-ī	रामतरोई	Ocra	ओक्रा
nīmbū (kāgjī)	नींबू (कागजी)	lemon	लेमन्
nīmbū (jam̐bhīrī)	नींबू (जँभीरी)	Lime	लाइम
Pudīnā	पुदीना	Mint	मिंट्
kukurmutta	कुकुरमुत्ता	mushroom	मशरूम्
pyāj	प्याज	Onion	ऑनिअन्
papītā	पपीता	Papaya	पपया
kelā	केला	Plantain	प्लेन्टेन्
ālū	आलू	Potato	पोटेटो
kon̐hḍā	कोंहड़ा	Pumpkin	पम्पकिन्
matar (harā)	मटर (हरा)	peas (green)	पीज़् (ग्रीन)
mūlī	मूली	Radish	रैडिश्
chachīn̐ḍā	चचींडा	Snake-gourd	स्नेक्-गोर्ड
nenu-ā, ghi-ā	नेनुआ, घिया	smooth-gourd	स्मूद्-गोर्ड
pālak	पालक	Spinach	स्पिनाच्
shakarkand	शकरकन्द,	Sweet-potato	स्वीट्-पोटेटो
ratālū	रतालू		
tamātar	टमाटर	Tomato	टोमेटो
śaljam	शलजम	Turnip	टर्निप्
methī	मेथी	Fenugreek	फेनुग्रीक्

Spices : मसाले

adrak	अदरक	Ginger	जिंजर्
kapūr	कपूर	Camphor	कॅम्फर्
kastūrī	कस्तूरी	Musk	मस्क्
kālī mirch	काली मिर्च	Black pepper	ब्लॅक् पेप्पर्
keśar	केशर	Saffron	सॅफ्रॉन्
khamīr	ख़मीर	Yeast	यीस्ट्
jāyphal	जायफल	Nutmeg	नट्मग्
jāvitrī	जावित्री	Mace	मेस
jīrā	जीरा	Cumin-Seed	क्युमिन-सीड्
tejpāt	तेजपात	Cassia	कासिआ
dālchīnī	दालचीनी	Cinnamon	सिन्नमन
namak	नमक	Salt	साल्ट्
mājūphal	माजूफल	Gall-nut	गाल-नट्
mircha	मिर्च	Pepper	पेप्पर
lava g	लवँग	Cloves	क्लोव्स्
Ilāychī	इलायची	Cardamom	कार्डमम्
sirkā	सिरका	Vinegar	व्हिनेगर
sonth	सौंठ	Dry-ginger	ड्राय-जिंजर्
saunph	सौंफ़	Aniseed	अनिसीड्
haldī	हल्दी	Turmeric	टरमेरिक्
hīng	हींग	Asafoetida	असाफोटिड़ा

Birds : पक्षी

panchhī,	पंछी,	Bird	बर्ड
pakṣī	पक्षी		
a dā	अंडा	Egg	एग्
aḍ-ḍā	अड्डा	Perch	पर्च
ghoślā	घोंसला	Nest	नेस्ट
choñch	चोंच	Beak	बीक्
pañkh	पंख	Wing	विंग्
par	पर	Plume	प्ल्यूम
pa ja	पंजा	Claw	क्ला
pinjaḍā	पिंजड़ा	Cage	केज़्
pūñchh	पूँछ	Tail	टेल्
abābīl	अबाबील	Sparrow	स्पॅरो
ullū	उल्लू	Owl	आउल्
kaṭhphoḍvā	कठफोड़वा	Wood-pecker	वूड-पेकर
kabūtar	कबूतर	Pigeon	पिजन
kalhans	कलहंस	Goose	गूज़्
kākā,tu-ā	का का तुआ	Cockatoo	कॉक्काटू
kālā kau-ā	काला कौआ	Raven	राव्हेन्
koyal	कोयल	Cuckoo	कक्कू
kau-ā	कौआ	Crow	क्रो
garuḍ	गरुड़	Eagle	ईगल्
gid-dha	गिद्ध	Vulture	वल्चर्

gauraiyā	गौरैया	Hen sparrow	हेन् स्पॅरो
chaṁgādaḍ	चमगादड़	Bat	बैट्
chīl	चील	Kite	काइट्
ṭiṭiharī	टिटिहरी	Lap wing	लॅप् विंग्
tītar	तीतर	Partridge	पार्ट्रिज़्
totā	तोता	Parrot	पॅरॅट्
nīlkanṭh	नीलकंठ	Magpi	मॅग्पी
peḍukī	पेडुकी	Dove	डव्
batak	बतक	Drake	ड्रेक
batakī	बतकी	Duck	डक्
bater	बटेर	Quail	क्वेल्
bayā	बया	Weaver-bird	वीवर्-बर्ड
bāj	बाज	Falcon	फॉलकन्
bulbul	बुलबुल	Nightingale	नाइटिंगेल्
murg	मुर्ग	Fowl	फाउल्
murgā	मुर्गा	Cock	कॉक्
murgī	मुर्गी	Hen	हेन्
murgī ka bachchā	मुर्गी का बच्चा	Chicken	चिकन्
murgī	मुर्गी	Poultry	पॉल्ट्रि
mor	मोर	Peacock	पीकॉक्
mornī	मोरनी	Peahen	पीहेन्
bhāradvāj	भारद्वाज	Lark	लार्क

śatur, murǵ	शतुर्मुर्ग	Ostrich	ऑस्ट्रिच्
śyeń	श्येन	Hawk	हाक्
sāraś	सारस	Crane	क्रेन्
Hans	हंस	Swan	स्वान
hirāmań totā	हिरामन तोता	Macaw	मकॉ

Beasts : पशु

ūn̐ṭ	ऊँट	Camel	कैमल्
kastūrī m iǵ	कस्तूरी मृग	Musk-deer	मस्क् डीअर्
kuttā	कुत्ता	Dog	डॉग्
kutiyā	कुतिया	Bitch	बिच्
khach-chaŕ	खच्चर	Mule	म्यूल्
khaŕgoś	खरगोश	Rabbit	रैबिट्
khaŕhā	खरहा	Hare	हेअर्
khuŕ	खुर	Hoof	हूफ्
gadhā	गधा	Ass, Donkey	ॲस्, डॉन्कि,
gāý	गाय	Cow	काउ
giĺharī	गिलहरी	Squirrel	स्क्विरल्
gain̐ḍā	गैंडा	Rhinoceros	रिनोसिरस्
goŕkhaŕ	गोरखर	Zebra	झेब्रा
gh́oḍā	घोड़ा	Horse	हॉर्स
ghoḍī	घोड़ी	Mare	मेअर्
chītā	चीता	Panther	पॅन्थर्

chūhā	चूहा	Mouse	माउस
chhachhūňdaŕ	छछूँदर	Mole	मोल
jaňgalī sū-ar	जँगली सूअर	Boar	बोअर
zabŕā kuttā	झबरा कुत्ता	Spaniel	स्पेनिएल्
ṭaṭ-ṭū	टट्टू	Pony	पोनि
teňdu-ā	तेंदुआ	Leopard	लेपर्ड
nevlā	नेवला	Mongoose	मॉङ्गूस
duḿ	दुम	Tail	टेल्
paśu	पशु	Beast	बीस्ट्
pa jā	पंजा	Claw	क्ला
pillā	पिल्ला	Puppy	पी
bakára	बकरा	He-goat	ही-गोट्
bakárī	बकरी	She-goat	शी-गोट्
bakárī kā	बकरी का	Kid	किड्
bachhā	बच्चा		
bachhaḍā	बछड़	Calf	काफ्
bachhiyā	बछिया	She-calf, Heifer	शी-कॉफ् हीफर्
bachheḍā	बछेड़ा	Colt	कोल्ट्
bachheḍī	बछेड़ी	Filly	फिलि
billī	बिल्ली	Cat	कैट्
billī kā	बिल्ली का	Kitten	किटन्
bach-chā	बच्चा		
bandaŕ	बन्दर	Monkey	मंकि

ban -manuś	बन-मानुस	Orangoutang	ऑरङ्ग् आउटॅङग्
bail	बैल	Ox	ऑक्स्
bāraḣ si gā	बारहसिंगा	Antelope stag	अंटेलोप स्टॅग्
bāraḣ si gī	बारहसिंगी	Hind	हाइंड्
bhālū	भालू	Bear	बिअर
bheḍ	भेड़	Sheep	शीप्
bhe̐ḍī	भेंड़ी	Ewe	एव्
bheḍī kā	भेंड़ी का	Fawn	फान्
bach-chā	बच्चा		
bhain̐sā	भैंसा	Buffalo	बफेलो
mā̐nd́	माँद	Den	डेन्
me hhā	मेढ़ा	Ram	रॅम्
mema nā	मेमना	Lamb	लॅम्ब
mūsā	मूसा	Rat	रॅट्
m ig	मृग	Stag	स्टॅग्
lomáḍī	लोमड़ी	Fox	फॉक्स्
lakaḍ bag-ghā	लकड़बग्घा	Hyena	हाईना
lan̐gūŕ	लंगूर	Ape	एप्
bāgh́, vyag	बाघ, व्याघ्र	Tiger	टाइगर्
śikārī kuttā	शिकारी कुत्ता	Hound	हाउंड्
sā̐nḍ	साँड़	Bull	बुल्
sābaŕ	साबर	Chamois	शॉम्वा
ṣāhī	साही	Porcupine	पोर्क्युपाइन

siyāŕ	सियार	Jackal	जॅकाल्
sin̐nḥ	सिंह	Lion	लायन्
sīn̐g	सींग	Horn	हॉर्न
su-aŕ	सुअर	Pig, Hog,	पिग्, हॉग्
su-arī	सुअरी	Swine	स्वाइन
su-ī-ś	सुईस	Porpoise	पॉर्पॉइज़्र्
hariń, hiran	हरिन, हिरन	Deer	डिअर
hāthī	हाथी	Elephant	एलिफॅण्ट्

Reptiles, Worms and Insects : सरीसृप और कीड़े-मकोड़े

ajgaŕ	अजगर	Boa	बोआ
kachhu-ā	कछुआ	Tortoise	टॉरटाइज़
Kachhu-ā (samudrī)	कछुआ (समुद्री)	Turtle	टरटल
kālā sān̐ṕ	काला साँप	Adder	एडर्
Ken̐chulī	केंचुली	Slough	स्लफ्
Ken̐chuvā	केंचुवा	Earthworm	अर्थ वर्म
Kekaḍā	केकड़ा	Crab	क्रॅब्
khaṭmaĺ	खटमल	Bug	बग्
Giŕ-giṭ	गिरगिट	Chameleon	कॅमेल्यन्
gahu-an sān̐ṕ	गहुअन साँप	Cobra	कोब्रा
gojaŕ	गोजर	Centipede	सेंटिपेड

gob́railā	गोबरैला	Beetle	बीटल्
ghaḍiyāĺ	घड़ियाल	Alligator	अलिगेटर्
ghon̐ghā	घोंघा	Snail	स्नेल्
chhiṕkalī	छिपकली	Lizard	लिझर्ड
jahaŕ	ज़हर	Poison	पॉइज़न्
jahaŕ kā dān̐t́	ज़हर का दाँत	Fang	फॅङ्ग्
chīn̐tī	चींटी	Ant	ऑण्ट्
jugńū	जुगनू	Firefly	फायर् फ्लाय्
jun̐	जूँ	Louse	लूस्
jon̐ḱ	जोंक	Leech	लीच्
zīn̐guŕ	झींगुर	Cricket	क्रिकेट्
ṭiḍ-ḍī	टिड्डी	Locust	लोकस्ट्
titlī	तितली	Butterfly	बटर्-फ्लाय्
dariyā-ī ghoḍā	दरियाई घोड़ा	Hippopotamus	हिप्पोपोटामस्
bich-chhū	बिच्छू	Scorpion	स्कॉरपिऑन्
machh́lī	मछली	Fish	फिश्
dīmaḱ	दीमक	White ant	व्हःइट् ऑण्ट्
machh́lī kā bachchā	मछली का बच्चा	Spawn	स्पान
madhumakkhī (naŕ)	मधुमक्खी (नर)	Drone	ड्रोन्
madhumakkhī (mādā)	मधुमक्खी (मादा)	Bee	बी

mendhaḱ	मेंढक	Frog	फ्रॉग्
mendhaḱ kā bach-chā	मेढक का बच्चा	Todpole	टॉड्पोल्
phan	फन	Hood	हूड्
phatan̐gā	फतंगा	Grasshopper	ग्रास-हॉप्पर
makḍī	मकड़ी	Spider	स्पाइडर
makḍī kā jālā	मकड़ी का जाला	Web	वेब्
mak-khī	मक्खी	Fly	फ्लाय्
magaŕ	मगर	Crocodile	क्रोकोडायल्
mach-chha	मच्छर	Mosquito	मॉस्क्विटो
bar-re	बर्रे	Wasp	वस्प्
reśam kā kīḍā	रेशम का कीड़ा	Silkworm	सिल्क् वर्म्
reśam kā kau-ā	रेशम का कौआ	Cocoon	कक्न्
līkh́	लीख	Nit	निट्
sān̐ṕ	साँप	Snake	स्नेक्
śa kh́	शंख	Conch	कोन्च
sīṕ	सीप	Oyster	ओयस्टर्
suphnā (machhlī kā)	सुफना (मछली का)	Fin	फिन्

Parts of the Body : शरीर के अंग

anāmikā	अनामिका	Ring-finger	रिंग्-फिंगर्
an̐gulī (pair̍ kī)	अँगुली (पैर की)	Toe	टो
an̐gulī (hāth̍ kī)	अँगुली (हाथ की)	Finger	फिंगर
an̐gūthā (hāth̍ kā)	अँगूठा (हाथ का)	Thumb	थम्ब
ān̐kh̍	आँख	Eye	आय्
ān̐t̍	आँत	Intestine	इंटेस्टाइन्
ōṭh̍	ओठ	Lip	लिप्
e hī	एड़ी	Heel	हील्
kandhā	कन्धा	Shoulder	शोल्डर
kan patī	कनपटी	Temple	टेम्पल्
kamar̍	कमर	Waist	वेस्ट्
kalā-i	कलाई	Wrist	रिस्ट्
kān	कान	Ear	इअर्
kānī an̐gulī	कानी अँगुली	Little finger	लिटल् फिंगर्
kān̐kh̍	काँख	Arm-pit	आर्म-पिट्
Kohni	कोहनी	Elbow	एल्बो
khop̍ḍī	खोपड़ी	skull	स्कल्

gardan	गर्दन	Neck	नेक्
garbh́	गर्भ	Womb	वोम्
garbhāśaý	गर्भाशय	Uterus	यूटेरस्
gaĺmuch-chhā	गलमुच्छा	Whiskers	व्हिस्करस्
galā	गला	Throat	थ्रोट्
gāĺ	गाल	Cheek	चीक्
gudā	गुदा	Anus	अनस
goď	गोद	Lap	लॅप
ghuṭnā	घुटना	Knee	नी
cham ḍā	चमड़ा	Skin	स्किन
chūchuḱ	चूचुक	Nipple	निपल्
chūta ḍ	चूतड़	Buttock	बटक्
cheh́rā	चेहरा	Face	फेस्
choṭī (bālon̐ kī)	चोटी (बालों की)	Braid	ब्रेड
Chhātī (marď kī)	छाती (मनुष्य की)	Chest	चेस्ट
chhātī (strī kī)	छाती (स्त्री की)	Breast	ब्रेस्ट
Jān̐gh́	जाँघ	Thigh	थाय
jigar	जिगर	Liver	लिवर्
jībh́	जीभ	Tongue	टंग्
jūḍā bālon kā	जूड़ा बालों का	Lock	लॉक्

joḍ	जोड़	Joint	जाइंट्
ṭhuḍḍī	ठुड्डी	Chin	चिन्
turjani	तर्जनी	Index-finger	इंडेक्स-फिंगर्
tal̕va	तलवा	Sole	सोल
tālu	तालु	Palate	पॅलिट
dā hh́	दाढ़	Jaw	जॉ
dā hhī	दाढ़ी	Beard	बिअड्
dā̃nt́	दाँत	Tooth	टूथ
dimāǵ	दिमाग	Brain	ब्रेन
dhamnī	धमनी	Artery	आर्टीरि
nakh́	नख	Nail	नेल्
nathunā	नथुना	Nostril	नॉस्ट्रिल्
nareṭī	नरेटी	Gullet	गलेट्
nalī (pair̕ kī)	नली (पैर की)	Calf	काफ
naś	नस	Vein	वेन्
nāḱ	नाक	Nose	नोज़्
nābhi	नाभि	Navel	नॅवल
paļaḱ	पलक	Eyelid	आय लिड्
paślī	पसली	Rib	रिब्
pōr (an̐gulī kī)	पोर (अँगली की)	Phalange	फलॅन्ज्
plīhā	प्लीहा	Spleen	स्प्लीन

pīṭh́	पीठ	Back	बॅक्
peṭ́	पेट	Stomach, Belly	स्टॅमक् बैलि,
peḍū	पेडू	Abdomen	अब्डोमन्
puṫli (ān̐kh́ kī)	पुतली (आँख की)	Eye ball	आय बॉल्
pesī (puṭ́ṭhā)	पेशी (पुट्ठा)	Muscle	मसल्
pair	पैर	Foot	फुट्
phephḍ́ā	फेफड़ा	Lung	लंग्
beraunī	बरौनी	Eyelash	आय-लॅश्
bāĺ	बाल	Hair	हेअर्
bān̐h́	बाँह	Arm	आर्म
bhaun̐h́	भौंह	Eye-brow	आयब्रो
madhyamā	मध्यमा	Middle finger	मिड्ल-फिंगर
masū hhā	मसूढ़	Gum	गम्
muṭ-ṭhī	मुट्ठी	Fist	फिस्ट्
mukh́	मुख	Mouth	मॉउथ्
mutrāśaý	मूत्राशय	Kidney	किडनि
mūn̐chh́	मूँछ, (मोंछ)	Moustache	मुस्ताच्
Yoni	योनि	Vagina	जादू
rī hh́	रीढ़	Back bone	बॅक् बोन
rōmkūṕ	रोमकूप	Pore	पोर
rovān̐	रोवां	Hair	हेअर
lalāṭ	ललाट	Forehead	फोरहेड्

lohū, khūń	लोहू, खून	Blood	ब्लड्
śiśna	शिश्न	Penis	पेनिस्
haḍ-dī	हड्डी	Bone	बोन
hathelī	हथेली	Palm (of hand)	पाम (ऑफ् हॅण्ड्)
han̐siyā	हँसिया	Collar-bone	कॉलर् बोन
h idaý	हृदय	Heart	हार्ट

Clothes and Wearing apparels etc. : कपड़े और पहनने के पोशाक

astaŕ	अस्तर	Lining	लाइनिंग्
al̥pākā	अलपाका	Alpaca	अल्पाका
an̐gaŕkhā	अँगरखा	Tunic	ट्युनिक
an̐giyā	अँगिया	Bodice	बॉडिस्
hāit (an̐grejī topī)	हैट (अंगरेजी टोपी)	Hat	हॅट्
an̐gochha	अँगोछा	Napkin	नॅपकिन्
āstīn	आस्तीन	Sleeve	स्लीव्
ūn	ऊन	Wool	वूल
kapḍā	कपड़ा	Clothe	क्लॉथ
kamaŕband	कमरबन्द	Belt	बेल्ट्
kamīj	कमीज	Shirt	शर्ट्
kambal̥	कम्बल	Blanket	ब्लॅड्केट्

kareṕ	करेप	Crepe	क्रेप
kaśmīrā	कश्मीरा	Cashmira	काश्मिरा
kām dānī	कामदानी	Diaper	डॅपर
kinārā	किनारा	Border	बॉडर
kińkhāb́	किनखाब	Brocade	ब्रोकेड
kiŕmich́	किरमिच	Canvas	कॅन्व्हास्
kot́	कोट	Coat	कोट्
gaddā	गद्दा	Cushion	कुशन्
gulubanď	गुलबन्द	Muffler	मफ्लर्
ghun̐ḍī	घुंडी	Loop	लूप्
ghū ghat́	घूँघट	Veil	वेल्
chādar	चादर	Sheet	शीट्
chikan	चिकन	Lappet	लँपेट्
chhin̐t́	छींट	Chintz	छींट्
jām dānī	जामदानी	Damask	डमस्क्
jālī	जाली	Gauze	गेज़्
jān̄hiya	जाँघिया	underwear	अन्डर वियर
jīń	जीन	Drill	ड्रिल्
jeb́	जेब	Pocket	पॅकिट्
ṭopī	टोपी	Cap	कॅप्
dup aṭṭā	दुपट्टा	Scarf	स्कार्फ
tāgā	तागा	Thread	थ्रेड्

tośaḱ	तोशक	Cushion	कुशन्.
tauli-ā	तौलिया	Towel	टॉवेल्
dareś	दरेस	Calico	कॅलिको
dastānā	दस्ताना	Gloves	ग्लोव्ह
dastī (rūmāl)	दस्ती (रूमाल)	Handkerchief	हॅण्ड्कर्चीफ्
duśālā	दुशाला	Shawl	शाल
nayańsukh́	नयन सुख	Jaconet	जॅकोनेट्
paṭ-ṭhā	पट्ठा	Lace	लेस्
pat́-lūń	पतलून	Pantaloon	पॅण्टलून्
pāy jāmā	पायजामा	Trousers	ट्राउज़र्स
pevan	पेवन	Patch	पॅच्
phatuhī	फतुही	Waistcoat	वेस्ट् कोट्
phalālīń	फलालीन	Flannel	फ्लानेल्
phītā	फीता	Tape	टेप्
baṭań	बटन	Button	बटन्
banāt́	बनात	Broad cloth	ब्रॉड क्लॉथ
makh́mal	मखमल	Velvet	वेल्वेट
maǵji	मगजी	Hem	हेम्
malmal	मलमल	Linen	लिनन्
māṭāpulām	माटापुलाम	Madapollam	माडापोलम्
mureṭha	मुरेठा	Turban	टर्बन्
mojā	मोज़ा	Stockings	स्टॉकिंग्स्

rajai	रजाई	Quiet	क्विल्ट
rafū	रफ़ू	Darning	डार्निंग्
rū-ī	रूई	Cotton	कॉटन्
reśaṁ	रेशम	Silk	सिल्क्
labādā	लबादा	Cloak, Gown	क्लोक्, गाउन्
la kī lāṭ	लंकिलाट	Longcloth	लॉङ्ग् क्लॉथ्
laha gā	लहँगा	Petti-coat	पेटी-कोट्
saraj	सरज	Serge	सर्ज्
sāṭaṅ	साटन	Satin	सॅटिन्
sāfā	साफ़ा	Turban	टर्बन्
sūt	सूत	Yarn	यार्न

Ornaments : आभूषण

aṅgūṭhī	अँगूठी	Ring	रिंग्
kaṅgan	कँगन	Bracelet	ब्रेसलेट्
karhā	कड़ा	Bangle	बॅङ्गल्
karhī	कड़ी	Link	लिंक्
karaṅ phūl	करन फूल	Ear-ring	इअर-रिंग्
kāṅṭā (bāl kā)	काँटा (बाल का)	Hairpin	हेअर्-पिन
kāṅṭā (sāḍī kā)	काँटा (साड़ी का)	Brooch	ब्रूच्
kīl nāk kī	कील नाक की	Nose-pin	नोज़-पिन्

chimṭī	चिमटी	Clip	क्लिप्
chūḍī	चूड़ी	Bangle	बॅङ्गल्
josań	जोसन	Armlet	आर्म्लिट्
tamagā	तमगा	Medal	मेडल्
tallā (kāń kā)	तल्ला (कान का)	Ear-stud	इअर्-स्टड्
toḍā	तोड़ा	Wristlet	रिस्ट्लेट्
nathunī	नथुनी	Nose-ring	नोज़् रिंग्
peṭī	पेटी	Belt	बेल्ट्
paijanī	पैजनी	Anklet	ॲङ्क लेट्
bājū band	बाजू बन्द	Armlet	आर्मलेट्
mālā	माला	Garland	गारलॅण्ड्
mukuṭ	मुकुट	Tiara	टिआरा
laṭkań	लटकन	Locket	लॉकेट्
lolak	लोलक	Pendant	पेंडांट्
sikḍī	सिकड़ी	Chain	चेन्
hāŕ	हार	Necklace	नेक्लेस
hansulī	हँसुली	Neckband	नेक़ बॅण्ड्

Jewels रत्न

gomedak	गोमेदक	Zircon	झिरकॉन्
javāhirāt	जवाहिरात	Gems	जेम्स्

nīlaḿ	नीलम	Sapphire	सफायर्
pannā	पन्ना	Emerald	एमरल्ड्
pukhŕāj́	पुखराज	Topaz	टोपाझ
poĺkī	पोलकी	Opal	ओपल्
phirojā	फीरोज़ा	Turquoise	टरक्वाज़्
billouŕ	बिल्लौर	Pebble	पेबल्
māniḱ	मानिक	Ruby	रुबि
mū̐ngā	मूँगा	Coral	कोरल्
moti	मोती	Pearl	पर्ल
moti kī sīṕ	मोती की सीप	Mother of pearl	मदर् ऑफ पर्ल
sulemānī	सुलेमानी	Agate	ॲगेट्
pat-ther	पत्थर		
laĥsuniyā̐n	लहसुनियाँ	Cat's eye	कॅट्स आय
hīrā	हीरा	Diamond	डायमंड

Relatives : सगे-संबंधी

mā̐n, ammā	माँ, अम्मा	Mammā	ममा
bāvā	बावा	Pāpa	पापा
mātā	माता	Mother	मदर्
pitā	पिता	Father	फादर्
put	पुत्र	Son	सन्
Putrī	पुत्री	Daughter	डाटर्

bhā-ī	भाई	Brother	ब्रदर्
bahan	बहन	Sister	सिस्टर्
chāchā	चाचा	Uncle	अंकल्
māmā	मामा	Uncle	अंकल्
dādā	दादा	Grand-father	ग्रॅण्ड्-फ़ॅदर्
nānā	नाना	Grand-father	ग्रॅण्ड्-फ़ॅदर्
dādī	दादी	Grand-mother	ग्रॅण्ड्-मदर्
nānī	नानी	Grand-mother	ग्रॅण्ड्-मदर्
pati	पति	Husband	हस्बॅण्ड्
patnī	पत्नी	Wife	वाइफ्
patohū	पतोहू	Daughter-in-law	डाट्र-इन्-ला
sāś	सास	Mother-in-law	मदर्-इन्-ला
sasuŕ	ससुर	Father-in-law	फ़ादर्-इन्-ला
bhāvaj́	भावज	Sister-in-law	सिस्टर्-इन्-ला
jeṭh́, devaŕ	जेठ, देवर्	Brother-in-law	ब्रदर्-इन्-ला
dāmād́	दामाद	Son-in-law	सन्-इन्-ला
uṕ patnī	उपपत्नी	Co-wife	को-वाइफ्
chāchī	चाची	Aunt	ऑण्ट्
māmī	मामी	Aunt	ऑण्ट्
bhatījā, bhā̃njā	भतीजा, भाँजा	Nephew	नेफ्यू
bhatījī, bhā̃njī	भतीजी, भाँजी	Niece	नीस्
sautelī mātā	सौतेली माता	Step-mother	स्टेप्-मदर्
sautelā bhā-ī	सौतेला भाई	Step-brother	स्टेप्-ब्रदर्

sautelī bahań	सौतेली बहन	Step-sister	स्टेप्-सिस्टर्
dattaḱ put a	दत्तक पुत्र	adopted-son	अडॉपटेड्-सन्
dattaḱ kanyā	दत्तक कन्या	adopted daughter	अडॉप्टेड्- डाटर्

Conditions of the Body and Ailments : शारीरिक अवस्था और रोग

aṇd́v id-dhi	अण्डवृद्धि	Hydrocele	हायड्रोसिल्
andhā	अन्धा	Blind	ब्लाइंड्
alṕd iṣṭi	अल्पदृष्टि	Short-sight	शार्ट-साइट्
amlápittá	अम्लपित्त	Acidity	एसिडिटि
atisāŕ	अतिसार	Diarrhoea	डायरिआ
āt́śaḱ	आतशक	Syphilis	सिफलिस्
ān̈kh́ ānā	आँख आना	Conjunctivitis	कंजंक्टिविटिज्
ān̈t́ utaŕnā	आँत उतरना	Hernia	हर्निआ
ān̈sū	आँसू	Tears	टिअर्स
ubāsī	उबासी	Yawn	यान्
okā-ī, vamań	ओकाई, वमन	Nausea	नॉसिआ।
ain̈chā	ऐंचा	Squint-eyed	स्क्विंट्-आइड्
kakhaurī	कखौरी	Bubo	बुबो
kaṇṭh́mālā	कण्ठमाला	Goitre	गोइटर
kaď	कद	Stature	स्टेचर

kapĥ	कफ	Phlegm	फ्लेम्
kai kaŕnā	कै करना (कय)	Vomit	वामिट्
kāmĺā	कामला	Jaundice	जॉन्डिस्
kālā jvaŕ	काला ज्वर	Typhus	टायफस्
kāś	कास	Bronchitis	ब्रॉन्काइटिस्
kānā	काना	One-eyed	वन-आइड्
kubḍa	कुबड़ा	Hunch-backed	हंच्-बॅक्ड्
ko hh́	कोढ़	Leprosy	लिप्रसि
koṣtĥbad-dhatā	कोष्ठबद्धता	Constipation	कॉन्स्टिपेशन
k mi	कृमि	Worms	वर्म्स्
khaśrā	खसरा	Eczema	एक्झिमा
khān̐sī	खाँसी	Cough	कॉफ
khūń kī kamī	खून की कमी	Anaemia	अनेमिआ
khuń bahna	खून बहना	Haemorrhage	हॅमोरेज्
gathhiyā	गठिया	Rheumatism	रयूमॅटिज़्म
garbhpāt	गर्भपात	Abortion	अबोर्शन
gaŕmī	गरमी	Syphilis	सिफलिस्
gaĺkā	गलका	Whitlow	व्हिटलो
galā baiṭĥnā	गला बैठना	Hoarseness	हॉर्सनेस्
gān̐ṭĥ	गाँठ	Tumour	टयूमर्
giĺṭī	गिलटी	Tumour	टयूमर्
gūn̐gā	गूँगा	Dumb	डम

ga jā	गंजा	Bald	बाल्ड
ghāv	घाव	Wound	वूण्ड्
chakkar	चक्कर	Giddiness	गिडिनेस्
chakotā	चकोता	Betch	बेच्
charbī ba hĥnā	चर्बी बढ़ना	Obesity	ओबेसिटि
choṭ	चोट	Hurt	हर्ट्
chhīnk	छींक	Sneeze	स्नीझ्
chhoṭā	छोटा	Short	शॉर्ट्
jalódāŕ	जलोदार	Dropsy	ड्रॉप्सि
javāń	जवान	Young	यंग्
Jaharbād	जहरबाद	Carbuncle	कारबँकल
jukāḿ	जुकाम	Coryza	कोरिझा
juḍī	जुड़ी	Ague	ॲग्यू
jambhā-ī	जँभाई	Yawn	यान्
jvar	ज्वर	Fever	फिवर्
ṭhaṇḍ	ठंड	Chill	चिल्
ḍakār	डकार	Belch	बेल्च्
ḍo rhā	डोंड़सा	Pimple	पिंपल
tandurustī	तन्दुरुस्ती	Health	हेल्थ्
thūḱ	थूक	Spittle	स्पिटर्ल
damā	दमा	Asthma	अस्थमा
darḋ	दर्द	Pain	पेन्

dard (sir' kā)	दर्द (सिर का)	Headache	हेड् एक
dast	दस्त	Diarrhoea	डायरिआ
dānt baiṭhnā	दाँत बैठना	Lock-jaw	लॉक्-जा
dād	दाद	Ringworm	रिंग्-वर्म
dublā	दुबला	Lean	लीन्
dūr d iṣṭī	दूर दृष्टि	Long-sight	लॉङ्ग्-साइट्
nas chataknā	नस चटकना	Sprain	स्प्रेन्
nāsūr	नासूर	wound	वून्ड
nīnd	नींद	Sleep	स्लीप्
nīnd na ānā	नींद न आना	Insomnia	इंसोम्निआ
pathrī	पथरी	Stone	स्टोर्न
pasīnā	पसीना	Sweat	स्वेट्
pāgal	पागल	Mad	मॅड्
pāgalpan	पागलपन	Insanity	इन्सॅनिटि
pitta	पित्त	Bile	बाइर्ल
pīk	पीक	Pus	पस्
pechis	पेचिस	Dysentery	डिसेन्ट्रि
pradar	प्रदर	Leucorrhoea	ल्यूकोरिआ
pyās	प्यास	Thirst	थर्स्ट
phil pānv	फील पाँव	Elephantiasis	एलिफॅण्टासिस्
phunsī	फुन्सी	Pimple	पिंपल्
pho hā	फोरा	Boil	बॉइल्
balgam	बलगम	Phlegm	फ्लेम्

bavāsīŕ	बवासीर	Piles	पाइल्स्
bahumūt	बहुमूत्र	Diabetes	डायबेटिज़
bāghī	बाघी	Bubo	बुबो
buḍ-dhā	बुड्ढा	Old	ओल्ड्
bukhār	बुखार	Fever	फिवर्
bevāý	बेवाय	Chilblain	चिल्ब्लेन्
baunā	बौना	Dwarf	ड्वार्फ
bhagandar	भगन्दर	Fistula	फिस्टुला
bhūkh́	भूख	Hunger	हंगार
mandāgni	मन्दाग्नि	Dyspepsia	डिस्पेप्सिआ
maroḍ	मरोड़	Griping	ग्रिपिंग्
mas-sā	मस्सा	Mole	मोर्ल
mahāmārī	महामारी	Pestilence	पेस्टिलेंस्
miŕgī	मिरगी	Epilepsy	एपिलेप्सि
mūt a	मूत्र	Urine	यूरिन्
moṭā	मोटा	Fat	फॅट्
motiyābind	मोतियाबिन्द	Cataract	कॅटॅरॅक्ट्
motīzarā	मोतीझरा	Influenza	इंफ्लुएंझा
mohāsā	मोहासा	Acne	ॲक्नॅ
laḱvā	लकवा	Paralysis	पॅरालिसिस्
lāŕ	लार	Saliva	सलिवा
viṣṭhā	विष्ठा	Stool	स्टूल्
rājayakṣmā	राजयक्ष्मा	Phthisis	थायसिस्

rog	रोग	Disease	डिसीज्
lang̐ḍā	लँगड़ा	Lame	लेम
lang̐ḍā bukhār	लँगड़ा बुखार	Dengue	डेंग्यू
lambā	लम्बा	Tall	टॅाल
lū-lagnā	लू लगना	Sunstroke	सन् स्ट्रोक
śītlā	शीतला	Small-pox	स्माल्-पॉक्स्
śvetkuṣṭh	श्वेत कुष्ठ	Leucoderm	ल्युकोडर्म
sān̐s	साँस	Breath	ब्रेथ
sūjan	सूजन	Swelling	स्वेलिंग्
sūrajmukhī	सूरजमुखी	Albino	ॲलबिनो
sūjāk	सूजाक	Gonorrhoea	गोनोरिआ
Sangrahṇī	संग्रहणी	Sprue	स्प्रू
svar	स्वर	Voice	वाइस्
svasth	स्वस्थ	Healthy	हेल्दि
hichkī	हिचकी	Hiecough	हीकॉफ्
haijā	हैजा	Cholera	कालेरा
kṣay	क्षय	Consumption	कंजम्पश्न

Musical Instruments : वाद्य

gha ṭā	घंटा	Bell	बेल्
cha g	चंग	Harp	हार्फ्
zān̐z	झांझ	Cymbal	सिम्बल्

daph́	डफ	Tambourine	टॅम्बरीन
dug dugī	डुगडुगी	Drum	ड्रम्
dholaḱ	ढोलक	Tomtom	टॉमटॉम
turahī	तुरही	Bugle	ब्युगल्
nagāḍā	नगाड़ा	Drum	ड्रम्
piyāno	पियानो	Piano	पिआनो
bañsurī	बाँसुरी	Flute	फ्लूट
belā	बेला	Violin	वायोलिन्
maśaḱ bājā	मसक बाजा	Bagpipe	बॅग् पाइप
muŕ cha ǵ	मुर चंग	Jew's harp	ज्यूज़ हार्प्
śaȟnā-ī	शहनाई	Clarion	क्लॅरिऑन्
sitāŕ	सितार	Guitaṙ	गिटार
sīṫī	सीटी	Whistle	व्हिसल्
hārmoniyam	हारमोनियम	Harmonium	हार्मोनिअम
taḃlā	तबला	Tambourine (small)	टॅम्बुरीन (स्माल)

Minerals and metals : खनिज और धातु

akīḱ	अकीक	Cornelion	कॉर्नीलिआन्
abhraḱ	अभ्रक	Mica	माइका
kaśkuṭ	कसकुट	Bronze	ब्रॉन्झ़

kasauṭī	कसौटी	Touch stone	टच्-स्टोन
kāँsā	काँसा	Bell-metal	बेल-मेटल्
kuruń	कुरुन	Emery	एमरि
koylā	कोयला	Coal	कोल्
(pat-thaŕ kā)	पत्थर का		
khaḍiyā	खड़िया	Chalk	चाक्
khān	खान	Mine	माइन॑
gandhaḱ	गन्धक	Sulphur	सल्फर्
gerū	गेरू	Ochre	ओक्कर
chak-mak	चकमक	Flint	फ्लिंट्
pat-thaŕ	पत्थर		
chāँdī	चाँदी	Silver	सिल्वर्
jastā	जस्ता	Zinc	झिंक्
tāँbā	ताँबा	Copper	कॉपर्
tutiyā	तुतिया	Blue Vitriol	ब्लू विट्रिऑल्
pakkā lohā	पक्का लोहा	Steel	स्टील्
pārā	पारा	Mercury	मरकरि
pītaĺ	पीतल	Brass	ब्रास्
rāँgā	राँगा	Tin	टिन्
shilājīt́	शीलाजीत	Stone's essence	स्टोन्स' इसेन्स
suŕmā	सुरमा	Antimony	अंटिमोनि
sa khiyā	संखिया	Arsenic	अरसेनिक्
sajjī	सज्जी	Fulleŕs earth	फुलर्स-अर्थ

sajjīkhāŕ	सज्जीखार	Natron	नॅट्रॉन्
sin̐ǵriph́	सिंगरिफ	Cinnabar	सिनाबर
sīsā	सीसा	Lead	लेड्
saphedā	सफेदा	White lead	व्हाइट् लेड्
sindūr	सिंदूर	Vermilion	व्हमिलिअन्
sa ǵmaŕmaŕ	संगमरमर	Marble	मारबल्
lohā	लोहा	Iron	आयरन्
haḍrāĺ	हरताल	Orpiment	ऑर्पिमिंट्

Trades and professions : व्यापार और व्यवसाय

akh́bār nabīś	अखबारनबीस	journalist	जर्नलिस्ट
adhyāpaḱ	अध्यापक	Teacher	टीचर
ahiriń	अहिरिन	Milkmaid	मिल्कमेड्
ahīr	अहीर	Milkman	मिल्कमॅन्
Injiniyaŕ	इंजिनियर	Engineer	इंजिनिअर्
kasā-ī	कसाई	Butcher	बुच्च
kārīgaŕ	कारीगर	Artison	आर्टिजन
kisāń	किसान	Farmer	फार्मर्
kitāb́pharoś	किताबफरोश	Book-Seller	बुक्-सेलर्
kun̐jḍā	कुँजड़ा	Vegetabler	वेजिटेबल सेलर
kulī	कुली	Coolie	कूली

koṭhīvāl	कोठीवाल,	Banker	बैंकर
		bainkar	बैंकर
khajānchī	खजाँची	Treasurer	ट्रैज़रर्
kharādnevālā	खरादनेवाला	Turner	टर्नर्
khudrā-pharosh	खुदरा-फरोश	Retailer	रिटेलर्
gandhī	गंधी	Perfumer	परफ्यूमर्
gāḍīvān	गाड़ीवान	Coachman	कोच्मॅन्
granthkār	ग्रन्थकार	Author	ऑथर
chiṭ-ṭhī rasān,	चिट्ठीरसाँ,	Postman	पोस्टमॅन्
		dākiyā	डाकिया
jar-rāh	जर्राह	Surgeon	सर्जन्
jahājī	जहाजी	Sailer	सेलर्
jādūgar	जादूगार	Magician	मॅजिशिअन्
jānchnevālā	जाँचनेवाला	Inspector	इंस्पेक्टर
jildsāj	जिल्दसाज	Book-binder	बुक्-बाइंडर्
julāhā	जुलाहा	Weaver	ह्वीव
jūtā banāne vālā	जूता बनाने वाला	Shoe-maker	शू-मेकर्
jauharī	जौहरी	Jeweller	ज्यूवेलर
tā-ip baiṭhāne vālā	टाइप बैठाने वाला	Compositor	कम्पोजिटर्
ṭāl vala	टाल वाला	wood-seller	वूड-सैलर

ṭhaṭherā	ठठेरा	Brassier	ब्रासीअर्
ṭhekedāṙ	ठेकेदार	Contractor	कॅन्ट्रॅक्टर्
ḍākṭar	डॉक्टर	Doctor	डॉक्टर्
ṫabalchī	तबलची	Drummer	ड्रमर्
tamolī	तमोली	Betel-seller	बेटल्-सेलर्
telī	तेली	Oil-man	ऑइल् मॅन्
tāntrik	तांत्रिक	Sorcerer	सॉरसरर्
raj	राज	Mason	मॅसन्
darjī	दर्जी	Tailor	टेलर्
dalāl	दलाल	Broker	ब्रोकर्
davāpharoś	दवा फरोश	Druggist	ड्रगिस्ट्
dā-ī	दाई	Midwife	मिड् वाइफ्
dant banane-vālā ḍaktar	दाँत बनाने वाला डाक्टर	Dentist	डेंटिस्ट
dūkāṅdār	दूकानदार	Shop-keeper	शॉप-कीपर्
dhāy	धाय	Nurse	नर्स
dhuniyān̐	धुनियाँ	Carder	कार्डर्
dhobin	धोबिन	Washerwoman	वाशरवुमन
dhobī	धोबी	Washerman	वाशरमॅन
nān bā-ī	नानबाई	Baker	बेकर
Kahār	कहार	Waterman	वाटरमॅन
parikṣak	परीक्षक	Examiner	एक्सामिनर्
pahiyā banāne vālā	पहिया बनाने वाला	Wheel-wright	व्हील्-राइट्

pahŕedār	पहरेदार	Watchman	वाच् मॅन
prakāśaḱ	प्रकाशक	Publisher	पब्लिशर्
Vyavasthāpaḱ	व्यवस्थापक	Manager	मॅनेज़र
pherīvālā	फेरीवाला	Hawker	हॅकर
photo	फोटो	Photographer	फोटोग्राफर
utāŕnevālā	उतारने वाला		
ba hha-ī	बढ़ई	Carpenter	कार्पेंटर्
bajāj́	बज़ाज	Draper	ड्रेपर्
bāiristaŕ	बैरिस्टर	Barister	बॅरिस्टर
bīj́vikretā	बीजविक्रेता	Seedsman	सीड्स्मॅन्
bhikṣuḱ	भिक्षुक	Begger	बेगर
Bhad bhūn̐jā	भूँजा	Parcher	पार्चर्
bhanḍārī	भंडारी	Butler	बट्लर्
machhu-ā	मछुआ	Fisherman	फिशर्मॅन
marmmat	मरम्मत	Repairer	रिपेअरर्
kaŕne vālā	करने वाला		
mallāh́	मल्लाह	Boatman	बोट्मॅन
māliḱ	मालिक	Proprietor	प्रोप्राइटर्
mālī	माली	Gardener	गार्डनर्
mīnākār	मीनाकार	Enameller	एनेमेलर
munīḿ	मुनीम	Accountant	एकाउन्टैन्ट
mudraḱ	मुद्रक	Printer	प्रिंटर्
munśī	मुन्शी	Clerk	क्लर्क

meh́tar	मेहतर	Sweeper	स्वीपर्
mochī	मोची	Cobbler	कॉब्लर्
modī	मोदी	Grocer	ग्रोसर्
mohaŕrir	मोहर्रिर	Writer	राइटर्
rasāyanī	रसायनी	Chemist	केमिस्ट्
raso-iyā	रसोइया	Cook	कुक
rokaḍiyā	रोकड़िया	Cashier	कॅशिअर
rańgsāj́	रंगसाज़	Painter	पेंटर
rańgrej́	रंगरेज़	Dyer	डायर
lād́ne vālā	लादने वाला	Carrier	कॅरिअर
lekhaḱ	लेखक	Writer	राइटर्
lohāŕ	लोहार	Blacksmith	ब्लॅक्स्मिथ्
vakīĺ	वकील	Pleader	प्लीडर्
vaidya	वैद्य	Physician	फिज़िसिअन्
ś́ikṣaḱ	शिक्षक	Teacher	टीचर्
sā-ī-ś	साईस	Groom	ग्रूम
sunāŕ	सुनार	Goldsmith	गोल्ड्स्मिथ्
saudāgar	सौदागर	Merchant	मर्चॅण्ट्
sańgtarāś́	संगतराश	Sculptor	स्कल्प्टर्
sampādaḱ	सम्पादक	Editor	एडिटर्
hajjāḿ	हज्जाम	Barber	बारबर
Haĺva-ī	हलवाई	Confectioner	कन्फेक्शनर्

Domestic Articles : घरेलू सामान

almārī	अलमारी	Almirah	आलमिरा
a gustānā	अंगुस्ताना	Thimble	थिंबल्
aṅṭā	अंटा	Bobbin	बॉबिन्
kaḍāhā	कड़ाहा	Cauldron	कार्ल्ड्रन्
kar chhul	करछुल	Ladle	लॅडल्
karābā	कराबा	Carboy	कार्र बॉय्
kanastaŕ	कनस्तर	Canister	कनिस्टर्
kanghī	कंघी	Comb	कोम्ब
tas'tari	तश्तरी	Tray	ट्रे
kursī	कुर्सी	Chair	चेअ-र्
konchnī	कोंचनी	Fork	फोर्क्
kīp (tīp)	कीप (टीप)	Funnel	फनेल्
kharal	खरल	Mortar	मॉ-र्टर्
okhalī	ओखली	Mortar	मॉ-र्टर
gāgar	गगर	Jar	जार्
gilāś	गिलास	Tumbler	टम्बलर्
chakla	चकला	Pastry-board	पॅस्ट्री-बोर्ड
chaṭā-ī	चटाई	Mat	मॅट्
chamachā	चमचा	Spoon	स्पून्
chalnī	चलनी	Sieve	सीव
chādar	चादर	Bed-sheet	बेड्-शीट्

chābī	चाबी	Key	की
pala ǵ	पलंग	Bed-sheet	बेड्-शीट
chiṁṭā	चिमटा	Tongs	टॉंग्स्
chıṁnī	चिमनी	Chimney	चिमनी
chūlhā	चूल्हा	Stove	स्टोर्व
chhaḍı	छड़ी	Stick	स्टिक्
a gīṭhī kī	अंगीठी की	Grate	ग्रेट
jālī	जाली		
chhātā	छाता	Umbrella	अम्बरेला
Ate ki chakki	आंटे की चक्की	Flour-mill	फ्लोर्-मिल्
ṭebal	टेबल	Table	टेबल्
ṭokrī	टोकरी	Basket	बॉस्केट्
desk	डेस्क	Desk	डेस्क्
ḍibbā	डिब्बा	Box	बॉक्स्
dhaknā	ढकना	Lid	लिड्
takiyā	तकिया	Pillow	पिलो
tarājū	तराजू	Balance	बॅलॅन्स्
tāŕ	तार	Wire	वायर
tālā	ताला	Lock	लॉक्
tālī	ताली	Key	की
tijorī	तिज़ोरी	Safe	सेफ्
tośak	तोशक	Matterss	मैट्रैस
tandūr	तन्दूर	Oven	ओवन्

thālī	थाली	Plate	प्लेट्
datuvan	दतुवन	Tooth twig	टूथ् टिवग
darpaṇ	दर्पण	Mirror	मिरर्
diyāsalā-ī	दियासलाई	Match	मॅच्
divālgīr	दिवालगीर	Bracket	ब्रॅकेट्
dhūpdānī	धूपदानी	Censer	सेंसर्
palanga	पलंग	Beds	बेड्स
pālkī	पालकी	Palanquin	पालन्क्विन्
pīkdānī	पीकदानी	spittoon	स्पिटून
phānūs	फानूस	Chandelier	शॉडिलिअर्
bakṣ	बक्स	Box	बॉक्स्
ba hhnī/zāḍū	बढ़नी/झाड़ू	Broom stick	ब्रूम स्टिक्
battī	बत्ती	Wick	विक्
bartan	बर्तन	Pot	पॅाट्
bāltī	बालटी	Bucket	बकेट्
belan	बेलन	Pastry-roller	पॅस्ट्रि-रोलर्
bench	बेंच	Bench	बेंच्
botal	बोतल	Bottle	बॉटल्
borā	बोरा	Sack	सॅक्
mathānī	मथानी	Churn	चर्न
masnad	मसनद	Bolster	बोल्स्टर्
mombattī	मोमबत्ती	Candle	कॅण्डल्

ras-sā	रस्सा	Rope	रोप
ras-sī	रस्सी	String	स्ट्रिंग्
rekābī	रेकाबी	Dish	डिश्
loṭā	लोटा	Bowl	बाउल
lo hhā	लोढ़ा	Pestle	पेस्टल्
śīśī	शीशी	Phial	फिऑल्
sandūk	सन्दूक	Trunk	ट्रंक
sarautā	सरौता	Nut-cracker	नट्-क्रॅकर्
salā-ī	सलाई	Match	मॅच्
sābun	साबुन	Soap	सोप्
sikadī	सिकड़ी	Chain	चेन्
si gār dān	सिंगारदान	Casket	कास्केट्
surāhī	सुराही	Pitcher	पिचर्
sū-ī	सूई	Needle	नीडल्
san̐ḍdasi	सँडासी	Pincers	पिंसर्स
hukkā	हुक्का	Hubble-bubble	हब्बल्-बब्बल